Simon Jackson. from
M & D.

Great Prints of the World

Also by the Author : PRINTMAKING

GREAT PRINTS OF THE WORLD

by

GABOR PETERDI

THE MACMILLAN COMPANY
COLLIER-MACMILLAN LIMITED, LONDON

Library of Congress Catalog Card Number: 69–10319

FIRST PRINTING

The Macmillan Company

Collier-Macmillan Canada Ltd., Toronto, Ontario

Printed in the United States of America

Acknowledgments

THE splendid cooperation of many people made this book a reality. So many have helped me that it would be difficult to list them personally. Therefore I would like to express my gratitude collectively to the curators and staff of the following institutions:

The Brooklyn Museum, New York
The Burndy Library, Norwalk, Connecticut
The Library of Congress, Washington, D.C.
Museum of Fine Arts, Boston
The National Gallery of Art, Washington, D.C.
The Lessing Rosenwald Collection, Jenkintown, Pennsylvania
The Art Institute of Chicago
The Metropolitan Museum of Art, New York
The Museum of Modern Art, New York
The Philadelphia Museum of Art
The Rijksmuseum, Amsterdam
The Yale University Art Gallery, New Haven, Connecticut

Special thanks are due Mr. Cecil Scott, who recently retired as editor-in-chief of the Macmillan Company, for his encouragement, and my dear friend Mr. Ken Purdy for his help with the manuscript.

GABOR PETERDI

Contents

Illustrations

WITH BIOGRAPHIES OF THE ARTISTS

Illustrations

Illustrations

Illustrations

Great Prints of the World

Illustration from Stradanus' *New Discoveries*, Printmaking shop. Engraving on copper, 8 x 10½. Issued early 1580. Burndy Library, Norwalk.

Introduction

AFTER one of my lectures, a woman from the audience asked me, "Do you think that printmaking is a major art form?" My answer was, "Do you think, Madam, that 'The Three Crosses' of Rembrandt is a major art work?"

This naively posed question has been put to me in various forms many times, sometimes aggressively stated as an opinion. I was truly amazed when I realized for the first time the existence of this widespread prejudice against printmaking, and I have tried to discover its origins.

The first and most obvious answer that came to my mind was the fact that a print is a multiple original. But then, so are many bronze sculptures cast in editions. Yet I have never heard anyone classify them as minor art works.

I also thought of the ancient practice of using skilled craftsmen to cut the wood blocks after a master's drawing. But how about the countless marble statues copied by stonecarvers after a small clay model?

The more I tried to rationalize this problem the less sense it made. Certainly some of the prejudice has its historic reasons. The printmaking of the seventeenth and eighteenth centuries was largely reproductive, yet, strangely enough, these centuries also produced some of the greatest printmakers, like Rembrandt, Seghers, and Goya. It is amusing that the very same people who will accept a photomechanically reproduced silkscreen print of a photograph as an "original painting" will sneer at a print. Yet we can't escape the fact that as soon as art became a commercial commodity it was classified by price. This established a hierarchy of values totally unrelated to any aesthetic considerations, with painting and sculpture on top, followed by tempera, pastel, watercolor, with drawing and prints at the bottom of the list. In contemporary art the introduction of countless new materials further complicated matters. An oil painting on paper is less valuable than an oil painting on canvas, but how do we rate the acrylic and polymer paintings?

[1]

The "special" treatment of prints by art historians and the often clannish attitude of "professional" printmakers contributed also toward the prejudice against printmaking.

Most art history books primarily deal with architecture, painting, and sculpture. Printmaking is generally ignored as it is not considered a part of the mainstream of art history. Printmaking has its own history and historians. The trouble is that most scholars don't accept printmaking as just another way of creating an image, and tend to over-emphasize its special character. Instead of writing the history of an art form they become involved in the historic development of a craft. Most books on the history of printmaking are heavy with pictures of the most mediocre reproductive stipple engravings, line engravings, mezzotints, just because they represent a highly skilled craft development of a certain period. Now, I don't say that this type of highly specialized study is not needed to train museum curators and art historians, but even so, it should be made clear that a print can be important only on the same basis as any other work of art, namely on its aesthetic value and its power of communication.

I am also convinced that the attitude of many "printmakers" who treat printmaking and the print as something rather special is harmful to their own cause. I don't think that printmaking is any more complex than painting and certainly not more involved with craft than sculpture. Yet, for some reason, one seldom hears painters or sculptors making a great fuss about their craft. To overemphasize the technology of printmaking can do nothing but serve mediocre artists, whose work could not stand up on its aesthetic merit alone.

At this point it may be appropriate to examine the problem of specialization in art. This volume is primarily devoted to great prints and printmakers. Who were they? Mantegna, Dürer, Goya, Degas, Rembrandt, Picasso, to name a few. They were not only great printmakers, but also great sculptors and painters. Above all, they were great artists. At times, a man can express himself better in one medium than in another, like the early masters of the woodcut or artists like Piranesi, Bresdin, and a few others. But they are more the exception than the rule.

Ideally, the artist should not accept the limitation of any medium. He should be as versatile as possible; he should select the best possible form of expression for what he has to say. This tradition in European art produced masters like Lautrec, Degas, Picasso, Matisse, Villon, Rouault, Kirchner, and Miró.

Considering the latest developments in contemporary art, the idea of specialization becomes even more undesirable. At the moment, there is so much interaction between the different media that conventional classifications are meaningless. Sculptors are involved with color, light, and motion, so are some painters. Canvases are shaped, and three-

[2]

TOSHUSAI SHARAKU, *Segava Kikunojo III as O-Shizu.* WOODCUT, 14⅞ X 9. BROOKLYN MUSEUM.

dimensional. Printed surfaces are integrated with painting. The print itself is becoming more and more sculptural, a heavily embossed paper bas-relief.

I decided to write this book for several reasons. The first was purely selfish. I always wanted to own a book filled with great prints. This is my book. I selected the artists and I chose their works. I did not include any print because it was historically or technically important, but because I found it aesthetically and emotionally satisfying.

This is an artist's book. I make no claim to objectivity. My judgment is based on my personality and on thirty years of intimacy with the printed image; thirty years spent not only in looking at prints, but in making them.

My first reason automatically touched upon my second reason to write this book. I hoped that by making a book that treats printmaking primarily as a significant visual expression I would counteract the widespread prejudice against printmaking and also prove that minor media don't exist, only minor artists.

I thought about this book for many years before I decided to write it. It is easier to dream about a lovely book filled with beautiful pictures than to sit down and try to work it out. First I had to face the fact that I couldn't possibly include all the prints I liked. I could easily fill a book with Rembrandt, Seghers, and Goya, another with Hokusai, Sharaku, and Utamaro, a third one with Schongauer and Dürer, and so on. I had to make hard decisions in limiting my material without losing the essense of my concept. This was a difficult, and at times a painful process. Yet, in some respects, it produced a more personal book by forcing me into more specific commitments.

The selection of my material was particularly difficult with artists like Rembrandt, Dürer, Goya, Hokusai, Picasso, and a few others. These masters produced so many great prints that to include all was out of the question. With these, my guiding principle was to select enough examples of their work to give a feeling of their total personalities and, if possible, to pick their less reproduced prints. This does not mean, of course, that I left out all famous prints. One could not leave out "The Three Crosses" of Rembrandt, for instance, without considerably distorting the significance of his *oeuvre*. At the same time I felt that including some of his small, rather earthy etchings would add to the total understanding of his complex genius.

I had to make another difficult decision: How much and what type of information should I include in this book. I did not want to make it a technical book; that would have contradicted my purpose. At the same time, I felt that to ignore completely the technicalities would be just as harmful as to overemphasize them. Many people still don't know the difference between an original print and a reproduction. Few, including collectors, and even artists, know how to take care of a print, how to mount it, and so on. Therefore,

[3]

KITAGAWA UTAMARO, PAGE FROM HIS BOOK ON WOMEN MAKING UP. COLOR WOODCUT, 14½ x 9¾. AUTHOR'S COLLECTION.

I decided to include all the basic information that I think useful to artists and collectors, as well.

I included a short biography of all the artists represented in this volume to serve as a background to their work. I also included a short historic outline to serve as a frame of reference to the content of this book. I want to make it clear, however, that I had no pretense whatever to write a scholarly book. This is art history, seen through an artist's eye.

Every artist included in this book was born before 1900. This was a very convenient cut-off point. It allowed me to include most of the great artists of the twentieth century but eliminated artists of my own generation. As I committed myself to include only important and significant prints in this volume, I felt that I had to have some perspective to form this type of value judgment.

This book is dedicated to all who love prints, to the appreciators, and to the makers, to collectors and to the artists, and last but not least to my wife who, with more love than patience, corrected my spelling.

History

THIS is a short sketch on the history of printmaking to form a backdrop for the outstanding man, the genius. I know it would be futile to enter into the endless argument whether history makes the great man or the great man makes history. The truth is probably a combination of both. Man not only reflects but also influences the intellectual climate in which he lives.

The history of printmaking is a good example of how new ideas are born both by chance and design. Many inventions had to be coordinated before the first truly printed image could appear.

The art of engraving is one of the oldest if not the oldest art form of man. There are many examples of incised designs dating from prehistoric times, on cave walls, on stones, and on bones. Even the idea of reproducing a design goes back five thousand years. The Sumerians used a hardened clay cylinder to press their cuniform writings into soft clay tablets. They not only had the idea of multiplication, but also a mechanical principle, the roller, which in more sophisticated form became the printing press as we know it today. In spite of this, several thousands of years had to pass before the Chinese and then the Egyptians made prints on textiles.

Three important discoveries had to be coordinated to make a print: first, to make a design on a hard material to print from; second, to make a material of sufficient size, flexible, and absorbent to print on; third, the pigments in liquid or paste form to print with.

On the basis of some stone designs and seals found in China, there is a speculation that the Chinese might have produced a primitive form of print as early as the second century A.D. As far as we know, the first wood-block prints on textile were made by the Egyptians in the sixth or seventh century A.D.

The first authenticated prints rubbed from wood blocks were Buddhist charms printed in Japan and distributed between A.D. 764–770.

[5]

The earliest printed image with an authenticated date is a roll of the Diamond Sutra printed by Wang Chieh in A.D. 686. It was found in the cave of the Thousand Buddhas in eastern Turkestan.

From time to time new discoveries extend the history of printmaking a few more years. Not long ago a printed book was found in Korea dating back to the eighth century A.D. But essentially the fact remains that in the context of known human history printmaking is a rather recent art form.

Printmaking in Europe developed centuries after it was known in the East. The first dated print in Europe was made in 1418 at Mainz in Germany.

Scholars still argue about the origin of the European print. The truth is impossible to determine, as the first prints—playing cards, and then the religious images—were transported from one place to another, and paper was imported. Thus, only the style of the drawing could possibly give some clue to their place of origin. I feel, however, that we should leave this speculation to the scholars as it has no relevance to our discussion.

Nearly simultaneously with woodcut printing, the dotted print (*manier crible*) or white line metal cut also came into existence. These metal plates were surface printed in the same manner as the woodcuts. Arthur M. Hind actually incorporated them into his history of the woodcut, instead of treating them as a transitional development of metal engraving. This is a debatable judgment, as I feel that the dotted print had a lot to do with the development of intaglio printed metal engraving.

The early fifteenth-century European woodcuts were simple and linear, a few textures here and there, but showing hardly any modeling of forms. Already in this period there may have been some division of labor between the designer and the cutter, but these prints are so well conceived within the character of the medium that I suspect that often the designing artist did the cutting himself.

As for the dotted prints, their style and craftsmanship definitely indicate that they originated from silver and goldsmith workshops. They were generally much more ornamental than the woodcuts, and many of the existing plates show holes in their corners to suggest that they were mounted as decorative panels.

Metal engraving and etching also originated in the decorative metalworking craft. The armormakers and goldsmiths worked with gravers and acids, and also rubbed pigments into their incised designs to observe the progress of their work. The idea of printing was only one step removed from this practice.

Vasari credits the Florentine goldsmith Maso Finiguerra (1426–64), with the invention of metal engraving. Unquestionably, he was the founder of the great Florentine school of engraving that produced many artists of stature, including the legendary Pol-

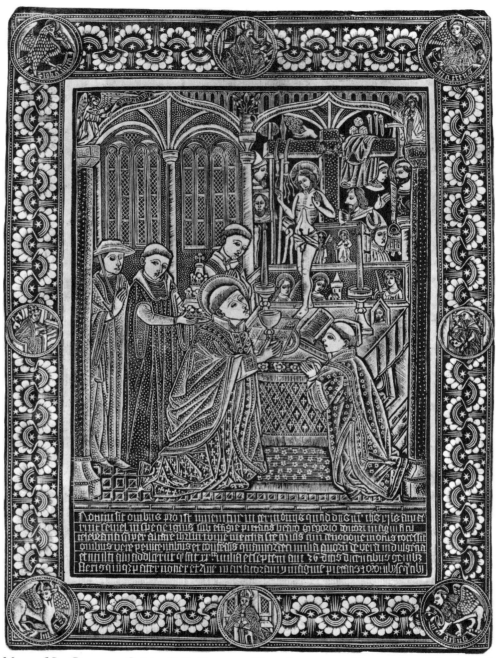

The Mass of St. Gregory. Crible, S. S. German, fifteenth century. Metropolitan Museum of Art, New York.

laiuolo (1429–98) who achieved his eminent position in the history of prints on the basis of only two known engravings.

But fifteenth-century printmaking was definitely dominated by Germany and the Lowlands. It is miraculous that so shortly after its introduction European printmaking could reach such heights. A long line of great artists appear, many of them unknown, or known only by their initials: Master E. S., Master I. A. M. de Zwolle, Master of the Hausbuch, Martin Schongauer, van Meckenem, Albrecht Dürer, Lucas Cranach, Albrecht Altdorfer, Lucas van Leyden, Hans Grien Baldung. In Italy, Pollaiuolo and Mantegna, in France, Duvet.

Most of the early woodcuts were colored by hand. Only in the second half of the fifteenth century was real color printing achieved by the introduction of the chiaroscuro (dark-light) method. In this process two blocks were used; one for color with the highlights cut out, and the black key block containing most of the linear details. The overprinting of these two blocks somewhat simulated the effect of a drawing on colored paper with painted white highlights. The earliest dated chiaroscuro print represents Emperor Maximilian on horseback. It was cut after the drawing by Hans Burchmair in 1508. Both Hans Grien Baldung and Lucas Cranach made fine prints in this manner.

Within a hundred years from its beginning, printmaking reached its zenith in Europe, and in less than another century it went into decadence and decline. This gradual erosion in the quality and creative vitality of printmaking started at the end of the sixteenth century and with some notable exceptions continued until the nineteenth century.

The reasons behind this are complex and a thorough analysis would have to take into account the changes in the social, economic, and religious situation during this period. It is worth remembering, however, that most prints of the fifteenth and early sixteenth centuries were religious images. Most of these were made for the Church and were promoted by the Church as part of its indoctrination of an illiterate populace.

Most of the early woodcuts were designed by an artist and cut by a craftsman, but the design was conceived as a print and was destroyed in the cutting process. Therefore, the process of making the printing block was reproductive, but the concept of the image was not.

The dotted prints and the line engravings were executed by the designing artist himself until about the end of the sixteenth century. Even artists of great stature like Dürer and Mantegna engraved their own metal plates, although Dürer's woodcuts were cut by someone else.

The drastic change in the artist's social and economic status brought with it a different attitude toward the print. It was impractical and below the dignity of a successful

Master E. S., St. George. Engraving, 6 x 4½. Gift of Mr. and Mrs. Potter Palmer, Art Institute of Chicago.

Renaissance master to spend innumerable hours in engraving a small metal plate. He could spend his time much more profitably by executing a commission for a large mural, or by painting portraits.

Many of these masters, Raphael for instance, were so much in demand that they couldn't possibly paint enough, even with the establishment of large workshops. It was therefore a logical idea for a highly skilled and commercially astute engraver like Marc-antonio Raimondi to start a very lucrative cooperation with Raphael. The engraved copies sold like hot cakes to the tourists who came to Rome to admire the paintings and the tapestries of Raphael. This was the beginning of a long period of commercialism that reduced printmaking into a reproductive art form and thus created most of the prejudice against the print.

In the seventeenth century, mezzotint (*maniere noir*) was invented by Ludvig von Siegen. This was a method roughing up the surface of the plate with sharp metal points and spiky rollers so that the whole plate would print black. The engraver then worked back toward the light areas by scraping and burnishing down the metal burrs. This method became widely used for reproduction after Abraham Blooteling perfected it. He invented the rocker, a serrated tool, to rough up the metal. Mezzotint lent itself perfectly to reproduction of paintings because with careful burnishing the engraver could achieve the most subtle passages of light. However, this medium didn't produce a single artist of real stature.

It is interesting to contemplate that within this period of decline emerged three towering figures in the history of printmaking: Seghers (c.1589–c.1638), Rembrandt (1606–69), and Goya (1746–1828). This phenomenon should lend weight to the argument that a truly great man will assert himself even under the most unfavorable circumstances.

At just about the time when the decline of printmaking started in the West, an astonishing new school of printmaking, the ukiyo-e (prints of the real world) began to flourish in Japan. It lasted until the nineteenth century and profoundly influenced the development of European art.

Until the seventeenth century the art of Japan was completely dominated by Chinese influence. The Japanese silk paintings of idealized landscapes, birds, and flowers, were hardly distinguishable from their Chinese counterparts. Then, in the seventeenth century, an artist of aristocratic origin, Iwasa Matabei, started to paint the "Transient World," and revolutionized the course of Japanese art.

This was the beginning of an astonishing period in the history of art. It produced one genius after another like Moronobu, Kiyonobu, Masanobu, Toyonobu, Harunobu, Shunsho, Itcho, Sharaku, Hokusai, Utamaro, and finally Hiroshige in the nineteenth century.

The Japanese aristocracy did not like the ukiyo-e print. Educated on the refined, idealized aesthetics of Chinese paintings, these prints, dealing with real people, actors, courtesans, and so on, seemed to them coarse and vulgar. The print in Japan became a

Hercules Seghers, The Landscape with a Crag. Etching, 4¾ x 6¾. Rijksmuseum, Amsterdam.

popular art, made for the people and loved by them. Prints were made as theater posters, as fan decorations, and wall decors, illustrating Japanese mythology, customs, and sex habits. Like the Greek vase paintings or the Mochic pottery, the Japanese prints became a total record of a people's way of life.

The Japanese print as a great art form was discovered by Europe. It influenced artists like Van Gogh, Gauguin, Toulouse-Lautrec, Bonnard, Vuillard, Matisse, and others. By the time the Japanese connoisseurs developed an appreciation for them, most of the great prints were in Europe, and they had to buy them back at high prices.

The Japanese color woodcut process is so different from the Western that I have to say a few words about it. The Western woodcut was partially reproductive, a facsimile process where the artist provided a completed drawing to the cutter. The Japanese print

Suzuki Harunobu. Colored woodcut. Bequest of Mrs. H. O. Havemayer, Metropolitan Museum of Art, New York.

was the result of a completely coordinated teamwork between the artist, cutter, and printer. The designing artist supplied separate drawings for all the color stages and he could see the completed image only after all the blocks were cut and printed. The original drawings were pasted on the wood block and destroyed in the process of cutting.

The interesting aspect of the Japanese print is, that although they have been called printed paintings, they always retained their graphic integrity. This was the result of a thorough understanding of the possibilities and the limitations of the media, acquired by the artists during long apprenticeships in masters' workshops. They had to cut blocks and print for years before they could become designers.

In Europe, the late eighteenth century produced a few more reproduction-oriented technical innovations: the stipple print, a tedious etching technique creating tones with little dots, and the stipple engraving or flick dot engraving, both somewhat resembling the half-tone effect of photoengraving.

Wood engraving was developed in England. In this method the wood block was cut cross-grain and not plankwise. This eliminated the problem of fighting the grain in the wood and allowed the usage of various gravers to produce a fine white line or texture. Thomas Bewick (1753–1828), the English illustrator, is considered the great virtuoso of this method but it was William Blake who produced the first wood engravings with real aesthetic significance.

The most important technical innovation of the late eighteenth century was lithography, developed by Alois Senefelder around 1798. This planographic printing method was based on a totally different principle from either the relief or the intaglio processes. (Description of method in glossary of techniques.)

In lithography, a well-printed image is the exact replica of the drawing on the stone. In that sense it is more reproductive than etching, woodcut, or engraving, where the method itself has a great influence over the character of the drawing. At the same time, lithography can be very direct and spontaneous and thus can appeal to painters who do not want to be involved with the special skills required to etch, engrave, or make a woodcut.

The first great artist to use lithography was the aging Goya, but it was Daumier and Toulouse-Lautrec who really explored its potentials most deeply. After them, many great painters used it and exploited its adaptability for color printing. It was extremely well suited to the temperament of artists like Bonnard, Vuillard, and Munch. Picasso also made several hundred lithographs, an important part of his staggering graphic output.

The nineteenth century was the great turning point in the history of art. Beginning with the seemingly pastoral attitude of the Fontainebleau school, a revolutionary process started that not only introduced violent aesthetic changes but eventually totally altered the philosophy of art.

With impressionism the modern era began with a bang. For the first time the avant-garde attitude became a conscious philosophical posture. From that period on, new ideas in art were introduced with ever-increasing tempo. The world was changing fast, and art changed with it. Technology changed the face of the earth, changed the life of its people, and communication spread the new ideas all over the globe.

In this great period of change, printmaking could not remain static. Experimentally oriented artists rejected the taboos of art history and revitalized the graphic arts. Two developments had direct bearing on the direction printmaking has taken since. One was the invention of photography and with it the photoengraving reproducing process, the second was the discovery of Japanese color-prints.

Henri de Toulouse-Lautrec, Femme Qui se Lave. Color lithograph, 20¾ x 16. Brooklyn Museum.

Printmaking as a reproductive process was made obsolete by the invention of photo-engraving. This set the stage for its exit as a craft and its rebirth as a creative medium.

The process of revitalization that started in the nineteenth century burst into a real creative explosion in the twentieth. To make an exhaustive analysis of all the reasons behind this would easily take a book in itself. In an oversimplified fashion we can credit two absolutely essential major factors: First, that important artists made prints again, secondly, that an ever-increasing popular interest in art created a market for it.

Already the first half of our century can take pride in a graphic output which for richness and quality compares favorably with that of the fifteenth and sixteenth centuries. The new developments in printmaking parallel the feverish innovations in all the visual arts. The last fifty years have seen more new ideas in the graphic arts than have the previous five hundred years.

It is hard to evaluate objectively your own time, to judge the significance of contemporary ideas. I am sure that most of the so-called "art" produced today will be forgotten in time. But then, we must remember that in any given period only relatively few men were gifted enough to create great art. Maybe today we produce more mediocre things because we are less selective. There is more of everything today, good and bad. This is the price of freedom. It is more important, however, that every man and every idea should have its chance.

The Original Print

THE lay public has always had difficulty in understanding what makes a print original. It has even more trouble in distinguishing between a reproduction and an original print. Generally, originality is equated with uniqueness, and the very nature of print, with the exception of a monoprint, negates this. In the last decade new developments in printmaking have further complicated this issue. Today even the experts disagree on what constitutes an original print.

In order to thoroughly understand this problem, we have to review its historic background. In the early fifteenth century the modern concept of originality did not exist. Most of the medieval artists were anonymous; they copied each other's style and often one artist appropriated another one's work and sold it as his own.

The earliest signatures were initials, like M. S. (Martin Schongauer) or Master E. S. These initials were used like the hallmark of the goldsmith, a guarantee for honest craftsmanship. This didn't keep van Meckenem from buying some of Master E. S.'s plates after his death and republishing them under his own signature. As we progress into the Renaissance, the artist becomes more and more an individual and the signature becomes more important. In 1505, Dürer undertook a long trip to Venice to stop Raimondi from copying his "Life of the Virgin" series, and selling them under the Dürer monogram. The only satisfaction he got was the stopping of Raimondi from using his signature.

Another important aspect to consider is that the early woodcuts developed as facsimile techniques involving two persons, the designer and the cutter. Although probably some of the very early wood blocks were cut by the designer, later on strict guild regulations actually forbade the artists to cut their own designs. At one point in medieval Germany there was a fight between the guilds whether the cutters should belong to the carpenters' or to the image-makers' guild.

Martin Schongauer, Christ Descending into Hell or Limbo. Engraving, 6¼ x 4¾. Clarence Buckingham Collection, Art Institute of Chicago.

One has to keep in mind, however, that no matter who cut the block, the design was explicitly created for the print and was destroyed in the process of cutting. This becomes a crucial issue when we try to establish various degrees of originality.

As we progress toward modern times, the artist's personal touch becomes more and more important, and with reason. If we compare the Dürer woodcuts cut by someone else with the metal engravings cut by himself, it is evident that the latter are more sensitive and more personal. It is noteworthy that they also command higher prices than the woodcuts. The Breughel engravings are even better examples of how much vitality and expressiveness is lost through the mechanistic cutting of a craftsman.

If any more argument were necessary to prove the superior quality of plates made by the artist himself, a quick review of the outstanding printmakers from the fifteenth to the nineteenth century would suffice. The engravings of Mantegna, Schongauer, and Dürer, the etchings of Rembrandt, and Goya, Seghers, and others, should be sufficient testimony.

The first copyright law was passed by the British Parliament in 1735 at the request of Hogarth, to protect him from plagiarism. From then on his engravings carried the line, "Published according to Act of Parliament." Thus the principle of copyright was established and soon introduced into most countries. Despite these and other protective laws passed since then, the artist is still rather defenseless. The custom of handsigned prints is recent. Whistler and Haden were the first artists to sign their names with pencil, on the margin of their prints.

In this review of originality I have to say a few words about the Japanese color woodcuts, as they represent a special category. The Japanese artist was trained as a cutter before he became a designer or a painter. The artist, the cutter, and the printer worked as a team. The designing was made in stages as part of a completely integrated creative process.

The development of mechanical reproduction was a boon to the graphic arts, but it also created new problems. The liberation of printmaking from reproductive functions helped its revival as a creative medium, but it also became a source of confusion.

A photo engraving and a line engraving are both prints. What makes one a reproduction, the other an original? This question seems childish, yet it isn't surprising if we keep in mind that through centuries handmade and handprinted line engraving was used to reproduce.

As printmaking became increasingly popular and lucrative, fraudulent practices further complicated the situation. These ranged from outright forgeries to simple mislabeling. In the United States this problem was the most flagrant with imported prints.

[18]

HENRI DE TOULOUSE-LAUTREC, *Au Moulin Rouge*. COLOR LITHOGRAPH, 18¼ x 13½.
BROOKLYN MUSEUM.

American printmaking developed along different lines from those in Europe and we simply did not have the skilled labor nor the equipment to help the commercialization of our printmaking. This is rapidly changing now, and is partially responsible for my decision to write this book.

Types of Frauds

1. PHOTOGRAPHIC REPRODUCTIONS of original prints, sometimes unsigned, at times bearing forged signatures. Fake intaglio prints are easier to detect than lithographs, although plate marks can be simulated. Close examination should reveal lack of embossment and mechanical screen in tonal areas.

2. HANDMADE REPRODUCTIONS of an existing art work (drawing or watercolor). These are more tricky as they can be real etchings, engravings, lithographs, woodcuts, etc., made by a craftsman, not by the artist. These fall into two subcategories: the first, made without the artist's knowledge and consent, the second, made with the artist's consent and signed by him. This second category is the most controversial as it is legally an original. The difference between this type of print and a Dürer woodcut, for instance, is that the former is the reproduction of an autonomous work of art, not conceived as a print, while Dürer made a drawing for the woodcut that was destroyed in the cutting process.

3. MISLABELING OF ORIGINAL PRINTS. The most common abuses fall into this category. The publisher sells a limited edition of one hundred in the United States but publishes the same plate also in Europe (perhaps with slightly changed color), and so on. Sometimes a signature is forged on an unsigned reprint. This is often done with the famous Vollard set of Picasso, as it multiplies its value. Look for the watermark of Vollard, as only the first edition has it.

4. REPRODUCTIONS SIGNED BY THE ARTIST. Although initially these might be sold honestly labeled, once they are in the trade they are often resold to uninformed people as original prints. With a little practice they are easy to detect: examined with a magnifying glass the mechanical screen shows clearly. One important bit of advice: unless you buy from a reputable dealer always take a print out of its frame as it is much harder to detect forgeries under glass.

    The print situation became so confusing that in 1960 the Print Council of America (an organization dedicated to the promotion and protection of original prints) felt that something should be done to correct it. I was sent as a delegate to the Third International Congress of the Plastic Arts, held in Vienna, Austria, to work out a resolution concern-

[19]

EDVARD MUNCH, *Nude with Red Hair*. 1901. LITHOGRAPH, 27⅜ x 15¹³⁄₁₆. GIFT OF JAMES THRALL SOBY, MUSEUM OF MODERN ART, NEW YORK.

ing the definition of "original print." The Congress appointed a special committee for this purpose and after long debate we drew up the following draft of resolution that was unanimously accepted.

DRAFT OF RESOLUTION
Adopted by the Third International Congress of Plastic Arts
Vienna, September, 1960

Original Prints.

1. It is the exclusive right of the artist-printmaker to fix the definitive number of each of his graphic works in the different techniques; engraving, lithography, etc.

2. Each print, in order to be considered original, must bear not only the signature of the artist, but also an indication of the total edition and the serial number of the print. The artist may also indicate that he himself is the printer.

3. Once the edition has been made, it is desirable that the original plate, stone, wood block or whatever material was used in pulling the print edition, should be defaced or should bear a distinctive mark, indicating that the edition has been completed.

4. The above principles apply to graphic works which can be considered originals, that is to say, to prints to which the artist made the original plate, cut the wood block, worked on the stone, or any other material. Works which do not fulfill these conditions must be considered "reproductions."

5. For reproductions no regulations are possible. However, it is desirable that reproductions should be acknowledged as such and so distinguished beyond question from original graphic work. This is particularly so when reproductions are of such outstanding quality that the artist, wishing to acknowledge the work materially executed by the printer, feels justified in signing them. . . .

It is evident that this resolution was intended only to apply to contemporary printmaking. Neither the International Congress of the Plastic Arts nor the Print Council of America have legal power to enforce them. The intention was solely to provide a code of ethics acceptable to most artists, museums, and print dealers.

I think that this resolution is a simple, straightforward statement on the most elementary requirement of the original print. Recent developments, however, proved it much more controversial than anybody suspected. Since the rise of the pop and op movement a great number of photographically produced silk screen prints have been published as originals. These prints do not qualify as originals under any accepted code, except that they are signed by the artist. The Print Council of America raised the question whether they should be accepted as originals and circulated a questionnaire to that effect. So far, the opinion of artists and curators is divided. Some say that nobody can dictate his working methods to the artist, and if he accepts a photomechanical method as original, then it is. Further, they claim that the character and style of these works calls for mechanical reproduction. I have a different opinion. I feel that the intent is not to dictate how the artist should work. I would resist and resent any such notion. Artists have the right to use any method they feel is the best to express their ideas. The problem is proper labeling. If one reproduces photomechanically an autonomous work of art, the result is not an original print but a reproduction. Limiting the edition or adding the signature of the artist does not change this. A proper label for the above described print would read: *Reproduction in limited edition, signed by the artist.* Thus the public would be honestly informed about the print. I feel very strongly that if we accept one photographically produced silk screen as an original, then we cannot object to any other reproducing method and in no time the market will be flooded with reproductions selling as originals.

Collecting Prints

I DISLIKE the word "collecting." I associate it somehow with an obsessive gathering of objects. People collect all kinds of things, from buttons to postage stamps. This type of involvement has more to do with possessiveness than with the love for a meaningful and individual creation. I believe in selection. The collection should develop organically as an outgrowth of a selective attitude. Indiscriminate accumulation of art can produce only a chaotic and unrewarding hodgepodge.

People buy art for many reasons. Love, status, and profit are probably the three major motivations. This is, of course, an oversimplification. I feel strongly, however, that in order to be a successful collector, an honest self-appraisal is necessary. If you buy art for profit, you have to think as a merchant. In this case you can't let your personal taste interfere with your financial judgment. The real amateur of art is driven by a passion not unlike the creative compulsion of the artist. To compromise between these two diametrically opposed attitudes would defeat both.

As an artist, I feel strongly that a print, just like any other work of art, should be bought only if it represents a meaningful visual and emotional experience. Museum curators are often guided by impersonal professional considerations. I consider this wrong as it tends to tolerate and even support mediocrity. Only committed people can build a meaningful collection. This takes courage.

What is the value of a work of art? Who could decide the "real" value of a Rembrandt painting or a Picasso print? This has nothing to do with the fact that when a work of art is for sale it becomes merchandise and its commercial value is determined by economic factors—by supply and demand.

Public interest in certain types of art work is influenced by taste-makers, museums, art critics, and not the least by dealers. Directly or indirectly they control the art market. Their backing can create demands for an artist's work. At times it is enough that an important museum shows an artist's work to drive his prices up. Past history seems to prove, however, that artificially inflated reputations do not last long, unless backed by genuine talent. A collector with personal taste and self-confidence has the great advantage that he can buy work that is not fashionable at the time, but has great quality for reasonable prices.

We are living in a period of unprecedented interest in art. As it is also a prosperous period, more people buy art than ever before. While formerly art collecting was restricted to a small group of extremely wealthy people, today many people of the middle income group buy original art. To the young collector and to any person with a modest income, the print is the most logical art form to buy. To the well-informed person, graphic work of high quality is available at reasonable prices. For hardly more money than the cost of a reproduction they can possess an original work of art.

Buying contemporary prints is less of a problem than buying old masters. The problem is not alone the price—some old prints of great quality can be bought for remarkably little money—but rather the more specialized knowledge necessary to avoid mistakes.

To the young collector interested in contemporary prints, there are print clubs and various organizations publishing contemporary graphic work for reasonable prices. Generally, for a nominal fee one can belong to these organizations and thus be entitled to buy any or all of their specially priced prints. Several of the print clubs publish prints by very well-known printmakers whose work published outside of these organizations sells for much higher prices. Generally these prints are smaller in size and printed in larger numbers than their regular editions in order to make the lower price possible. This has no bearing on the prints' quality as most modern plates or blocks can produce many more prints than the customary edition number (fifty to two hundred).

Numbering Prints

The number of prints making up an edition is decided by the artist or by an agreement between the artist and the publisher. The number is usually determined by two practical considerations: how many good proofs can be printed from the plate and how many prints can be sold. Usually the latter is the deciding factor as most plates can produce many more good proofs than the average edition number.

As a generally accepted practice in contemporary printmaking, the edition number appears on the lower left-hand corner of the margin. It consists of two numbers, the first giving the proof number, then, separated by a dash, the edition number. For instance, 1–50 would mean first proof in an edition of fifty. Collectors prefer to buy prints with a low edition number, and no. 1 is considered a prize. This is based on the mistaken notion that the lower its number, the better the proof. While this notion might have some validity if a drypoint plate were not steel-faced, it is otherwise unrealistic. Artists operate on the principle that the edition number shouldn't exceed the number of perfect proofs a plate can produce. Besides, the proof numbers seldom represent the sequence in which they were printed. When the printing of the edition is finished, and the prints are dried and flattened, they are reshuffled so many times that the printing order is lost by the time the artist numbers them.

This numbering procedure applies only to modern prints beginning approximately at the end of the nineteenth century. Regulated publishing started toward the end of the seventeenth century, but in the eighteenth century artists like Hogarth introduced a really professional attitude in publishing print editions.

State Proofs or Trial Proofs

These refer to proofs the artist makes while working on the plate to observe its progress. As they don't represent the finished art work, they are not part of the regular edition. These proofs are interesting documents as they show the artist's working method and they are helpful in gaining insight into the creative process. The various stages of a painting are destroyed by each successive step and lost forever. The printmaker has this unique opportunity to preserve a complete record of his working process. Trial proofs can be very valuable, sometimes even more than the finished work, as they may represent a visually exciting stage in addition to their uniqueness and historic value. Good examples are the state proofs of Rembrandt's "Christ Presented to the People" and "The Three Crosses."

Artist Proofs

When an artist sells a complete edition to a publisher, he has the right to pull a few proofs, outside of the regular edition, for his own personal use. These are marked and numbered as "artist's proofs." Although there are no hard rules to regulate these, it became customary to allow approximately 10 per cent on a normal edition (not more than one hundred) and 5 per cent on a large one (approximately two hundred).

In recent years there has been a great deal of abuse of this privilege. Some artists, confronted with the unexpected success of a print, could not resist the temptation of additional sales and issued artist proofs in excess of the customary 10 per cent. In one extreme case, the artist proofs exceeded the number of the regular edition. For this reason many people feel that the artist proofs should be incorporated into the regular edition number, thus the buyer would be informed of the total edition number.

Hors de Commerce marked H.C.

This is a device quite similar to the artist proof to distinguish the prints pulled for the private use of the artist or publisher. Originally, it was used to designate copies sent to critics, publications, gifts to friends and family; now it is often used to pad editions.

Signing of Prints

Contemporary prints are generally signed in pencil on the lower right corner of the margin. There are some exceptions. Picasso, for instance, sometimes signs in the center with red water color. On old prints, monograms or any other information about the print was engraved or etched on the plate itself. Below are some of the abbreviations from Latin often appearing on the margin of old prints:

Del. (Delineavit): The designer has drawn it.
Exc. (Exudit): The publisher published it.
Fec. (Fecit): Made it, engraved it, etc.
Imp. (Impressit): Printed it.
Inv. (Invenit): The designer designed it.
Pinx. (Pinxit): Painted it.
Sculp. (Sculpsit): Engraved it.

Canceling the Plate

Since the nineteenth century, the practice has been to cancel the printing plate after the edition is finished. Canceling means to alter the plate either by marking up its surface or altering its shape. This eliminates fraudulent reprintings. Unfortunately, this custom is not followed by every artist.

Some artists, including myself, feel that the plate itself is a work of art and should not be destroyed. One can avoid this and still cancel the plate by slightly changing the corners or by engraving a small mark on it. Some well-known prints have been republished after cancellation and are worth buying at a much lower price than the first edition.

Buying Contemporary Prints

Buy what you like but before you buy, do a great deal of looking. There are no short cuts. Taste develops by exposure. There are sufficient number of large print exhibitions and galleries handling graphics, excluding museums and other permanent collections, to offer ample opportunities to learn.

The price range of contemporary graphics is comparable to old prints. From $50 to $50,000 there is an incredibly wide selection, not only in price but also in style and, of course, in quality. The contemporary print market is fairly well regulated and it isn't too difficult to find out the approximate market value of a print. The work of famous artists represents an international commodity and is controlled as such. Dealers follow the market all over the world and thus the prices in Europe are about the same as in the United States. The only area where the collector runs a risk is in the quality of the prints he buys but in this he has to rely on his own judgment and taste.

My advice to the young collector is to start with reasonably priced prints by lesser known contemporary artists. This is a reasonable method to avoid costly mistakes. A big name and a high price are not always synonymous with quality. The work of many famous artists is very uneven. It makes a big difference which Picasso or Chagall print you buy. I am against buying art for financial reasons but I can't ignore the fact that an expensive art work is also an investment. Paradoxically, the collector whose prime concern is quality does better than bargain hunters.

I discussed fraudulent practices in the print world in my chapter on original prints. The only defense against these is knowledge or buying only from reputable dealers.

Buying Old Prints

The buying of old prints is a much more complex problem. The uninformed layman can very easily be misled. The value of an old master print is determined by many factors, at times totally unrelated to its artistic value. The price variations can be staggering even within the works of one master. Recently the "Hundred Guilder Print" of Rembrandt was sold in an auction for over $50,000. At the same time, a friend of mine bought "The Adoration of Shepherds" for $200.

The most important factors influencing the value of an old master print are:

1. The importance of the print.
2. The quality of the printing.

3. The physical condition of the print.
4. The rarity of the print.
5. The previous owner of the print.

1. THE IMPORTANT PRINT. Most great masters made a few exceptionally important prints. At times, art historians, critics, and collectors agree on specific prints as representative of high points in the artist's total *oeuvre*. There is a lot written about these works and they are frequently reproduced. Most museums and important collections want to have these prints and compete for them if they appear on the market. This inevitably drives their price way up. As most of these prints end in permanent collections, they are rarely sold. This further increases their value. Examples: Dürer's "Melancholia"; Rembrandt's "The Three Crosses"; Hokusai's "Big Wave."

2. THE QUALITY OF THE PRINTING. The printing on most old prints is very uneven. This is partly due to lack of good equipment but mostly to the tear and wear caused by mishandling. Thus a rich, evenly printed proof has much greater value than a faded or uneven print. To judge these you need experience. Before buying an important old print it is wise to look at a good proof of the same in a museum collection.

3. THE PHYSICAL CONDITION OF THE PRINT. The printing condition is already covered in point two. The condition of the paper is another important factor influencing value. Unfortunately, most old prints were subjected to all kinds of abuse. It is rare to find an old print in perfect condition. Most of them have little margin or they are trimmed right up to the plate mark. Although it has no effect on the aesthetic quality of the print, a full margin increases its value considerably.

Most old prints have been repaired. This is hard to spot when it is well done by a professional. Holding the print up against the light is the easiest way to discover repairs. Again, this might not affect the artistic qualities of the print, only its commercial value.

Examine the paper for discolorations caused by dampness or fungi. Look for tiny holes that can be caused by silverfish, termites, woodworms, book lice, etc. These conditions would considerably reduce the value of a print. Sometimes the print has to be treated by an expert to prevent further deterioration.

4. THE RARE PRINT. To some extent I covered this in point one. The important print is generally also the rare one, but sometimes the reverse can happen. A print becomes important because it is rare. For instance, even a minor print made by the Master of the Amsterdam Cabinet is important and very expensive, because all his prints are rare.

5. THE PREVIOUS OWNER OF THE PRINT. If a print was owned previously by a famous collector it will sell for a higher price than a print of the same quality sold by an unknown. People love celebrities and the fame of the previous owner adds to the glamour of the

print. Important collectors and museums have their own stamp. Often by tracing the stamp marks one can track down the origin of the print. If you care to place your own stamp on your prints, be careful to use only special printing ink that won't penetrate the paper. Place your mark on the back as far off the image as possible.

For anybody interested in tracing down a collector's mark there is a catalogue assembled by Fritz Lugt. It is entitled *Les Marques de Collections*, and was published in Amsterdam in 1921.

Catalogue References

Most old master prints are catalogued. In these publications one can find a complete description, including date, dimensions, technique, size of the edition, or the number of known proofs in existence. Most of the recent *Catalogue Raisonne* also includes reproductions.

The most important catalogue is Adam Bartsch's *Le Peintre-graveur* in twenty-one volumes published in Vienna (1803–21). Quite often the Bartsch number appears in a catalogue after the print's title.

Since this catalogue many others have appeared, as this is a continuous process.

A. P. G. Robert-Dumesnil, *Peintre graveur français.* (Paris, Warée, 1835–71.) 11 vols.
Alessandro Baudi di Vesme, *La peintre-graveur italien.* (Milan, Hoepli, 1906.)
Alfred von Wurzbach, *Niederländisches Künstler Lexikon.* (Wien, Halm, 1906–11.) 3 vols.
Henri Beraldi, *Les graveurs du XIXe siècle.* (Paris, Conquet, 1885–92.) 12 vols.
Loys Delteil, *Le peintre-graveur illustré (XIXe et XXe siècles).* (Paris, Chez l'auteur, 1906–30.) 31 vols. (Reprint edition in preparation. Amsterdam, Israel, 1968.)
Arthur Mayger Hind, *Engraving in England in the sixteenth and seventeenth centuries; a descriptive catalogue with introductions.* (Cambridge, Univ. Press, 1952–55.) 2 vols.; *Early Italian engraving, a critical catalogue with complete reproduction of all the prints described* . . . (London, Quaritch; N. Y., M. Knoedler & Co., 1938–48.) 7 vols.
Max Lehrs, *Geschichte und kritischer Katalog des deutschen, niederländischen und französischen Kupferstichs im XV. Jahrhundert.* (Wien, Gesellschaft für vervielfältigende Kunst, 1908–34.) 9 vols.
Georg K. Nagler: *Neves Allgemeines künster lexicon . . . Unveränderter abdruch der ersten auflage 1835–52.* (Leipzig, Schwarzenber & Schuman, 1924.) 25 vols.

Restrikes or Reprints

These are prints made after the original edition was issued, often long after the artist's death. There are many types of reprints and they represent a difficult and confusing situation. Contemporary reprints of old masters are fairly easy to spot; if nothing else the paper itself should give them away. There are many restrikes in the legitimate print market. A publisher can buy the plates of an old master and issue restrikes in unlimited numbers. These are sold as such for reasonable prices. Usually their print quality is poor as the plates are worn and steel-faced. So long as these are not misrepresented, one can't quarrel with them. At times, however, these are printed on old paper and passed off as originals. You must have knowledge and a good eye to spot these.

It is much more difficult and sometimes impossible to detect restrikes made in the same period the artist lived. I have already mentioned the Master E. S. plates reprinted by van Meckenen. Several of Rembrandt's plates were reworked and reprinted by his students. Even museum collections are full of prints of questionable origin. Museum curators are continually busy in revising attributions.

Examining the watermarks of the paper is one of the most reliable ways to determine the authenticity of fifteenth- and sixteenth-century prints. Briquet's *Dictionary of Watermarks* (Geneva) is the best reference book on this subject.

I would like to sum up this chapter with the reminder that commercial value and spiritual meaning are two different things. One should not be confused with the other. The price of a print and its intrinsic value are not always in direct relation.

The Mounting and Care of Prints

Very few people know how to display prints and how to take care of them properly. In this respect, unfortunately, professional people are just as frequent offenders as laymen. Museum curators are often horrified to see how artists mistreat their own work. I have had enough bad experience with frame-makers myself to realize the need of education in this direction. It is heartbreaking to see a great master's print glued to a cheap cardboard, or the border of a fine print ruined with masking tape. In this short chapter I will attempt to cover some of the most important rules that every artist and collector should know.

The Handling of Prints

Paper is fragile, particularly old paper. Handle it as little as possible. Mount the print as soon as possible to protect it. For permanent mounting always use pure rag boards; wood-pulp boards burn and discolor the print.

Do not pick up a print with one hand, this might put too much stress on the paper and break it.

Do not trim a print. It should be preserved as nearly intact as possible. If the print's edge is torn, it can be restored. Place it between two cardboards for protection and take it to a restorer as soon as possible.

Protection of the Print Surface

The surface of a print is delicate, rubbing might permanently injure it. Intaglio prints are particularly sensitive. Don't stack them without protective layers of paper between them. For this purpose tissue paper or glassine papers are the best. Lucite envelopes, which are also used, are a good but expensive protection. Do not use celluloid, it can injure the paper. Low-grade wood-pulp papers like newsprint should not be used, as the acid content in these might burn the print.

Framed or unframed, don't expose a print to extensive sunlight. Sunlight can be very dangerous to color prints as very few colors are stable enough to withstand a long exposure to light. Japanese color prints are particularly sensitive.

Mat Board

As I said before, a permanent mat should always be pure rag board. Beside its acid content, the wood-pulp board can also harbor cellulose degenerating bacteria and when damp might develop fungi.

Mat Construction

A properly constructed mat consists of two parts, the backing board to support the print and the covering frame to display it. The covering frame should be hinged with linen tape to the backing board. This allows the framing board to be lifted to examine the print if necessary.

Mat boards come in various thicknesses: one-ply, two-ply, and four-ply. The thickness selected has to be in relation to the size of the mat. For a small print two-ply is thick enough, but in most cases four-ply is preferable. For display four-ply should be used, but if one has to store a great number of prints, the two-ply saves both space and money.

The width of the mat frame and the dimensions of the print has to be related. The mat should not overpower the image. A bold print can support a wider mat than a delicate one. Some people prefer the same width all around, others like to make the bottom margin wider. This is a matter of taste. If one mats for protective purposes to store the print, then standard proportions are the most practical. The sizes most commonly used by museums are: 30″ x 40″, 22″ x 28″, 16″ x 22″, 14″ x 18″. Until fairly recently, most big shows insisted on standard mat sizes and museums were reluctant to buy odd size prints because this represented a storage problem. This attitude has changed now, because it eliminated too many important contemporary prints.

The window size of a mat should always be slightly larger than the printed image itself, generally one-half-inch all around, possibly a little more on the bottom if the print is signed. Many old prints have little or no border. They should float in the mat opening. Don't cover any part of the print.

The mounting of contemporary prints often represents special problems. In many respects the window mat is the equivalent of the old-fashioned frame. The space concept of most abstract art is contradictory to framing. Abstract prints look better floating, (tipped to the surface) than in a window mat. To frame these, one should use hardly visible metal or plastic molding.

The heavily embossed sculptural print represents another problem. They have to be displayed in specially constructed shadow-box type frames, in order to protect the relief. In storage they should never be piled up flat, as this would crush the embossment.

Hinging of Prints

Most prints are injured by affixing them incorrectly to the background. They should be hinged and not glued. If the print is stored, it can be hinged from the side for easier handling. If the print is framed or displayed in vertical position, it should be hinged from

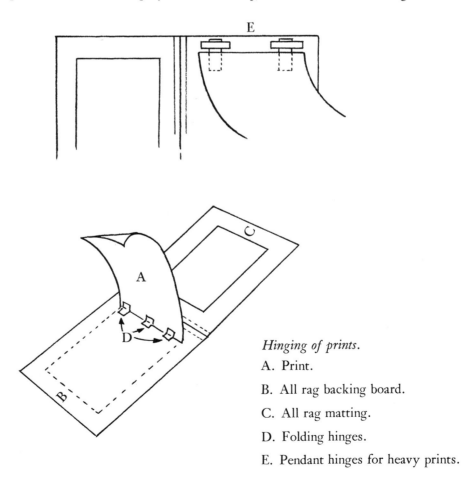

Hinging of prints.
A. Print.
B. All rag backing board.
C. All rag matting.
D. Folding hinges.
E. Pendant hinges for heavy prints.

the top. Small prints can be hinged from the corners, but large prints need more support. Use only safe materials. Never use adhesive tapes, gummed paper tapes, Scotch tape, or masking tape. These tend to deteriorate, discolor, and stain the paper. The best material for hinges is a sheer but strong paper. Most of the Japanese papers are excellent for this purpose. The hinging paper never should be stronger than the print itself. Thus, under stress, the hinge would tear, not the print. To affix the hinges, do not use glues, rubber cement, or any other synthetic adhesive. Nothing should be used that would penetrate into the paper and stain it. White library paste is the least harmful, but rice starch mixed with water is best.

Framing of Prints

Framing has two functions: display and protection. A frame is bought to show the print and not itself. An over-rich, gaudy, or heavy frame intrudes into the aesthetic experience. The frame should be simple, strong enough to hold the glass and to protect the print.

Unfortunately, prints have to be displayed under glass. I say unfortunately because glass doesn't enable one to experience fully the tactile qualities of the print, but to exhibit prints for any length of time without protection can cause permanent damage. The best glass is specially manufactured for pictures. It is thinner than window glass. It does not distort color and it is lighter. There is a special glare-proof glass also, but I don't like it. Because of its gray tint, it is particularly unsuited for color prints. In recent years plexiglass is often used for extra large prints. Its advantages are lightness and unbreakability. Unfortunately plexiglass scratches very easily and must be coated with antistatic compound because it attracts dust. Prints should be kept from direct contact with the glass. Frequent temperature changes in damp climate may cause condensation. Water-stained paper is more vulnerable to microbiological attack and the print might develop fungi. The simplest protection is a deep enough pure rag mat. If this is not enough, a filler should be inserted into the frame to increase the space between the mat and the glass. This always has to be done with "floated" prints.

If possible, the backboard of the frame should also be rag or rag faced. The back of the frame should be sealed with tape to eliminate the penetration of dust. In damp climates it is advisable to deep the frame away from the wall by placing corks on its four corners. This facilitates the free circulation of air. It goes without saying that air conditioning and humidity control are the ideal protections against the hazards of climate.

No matter how much a print may buckle due to atmospheric conditions, do not press it, iron it, stretch it, and especially do not glue it down. Many great prints have been ruined by this type of treatment.

[33]

Major Techniques of Printmaking

THE techniques of printmaking are divided into four major categories: relief processes, incised processes, planographic processes, and stencil processes. These are general categories and each of these have many variations, depending on the materials and tools used, and the way they are printed. The following paragraphs describe the major characteristics and possible variations of these processes. In addition, each technique or method of printing is related to a creative concept. A glossary will follow this general introduction in which important terms and techniques of printmaking are covered.

Relief Processes

The basic principle is to cut or etch away part of the printing block or plate (wood, linoleum, metal, plastic, etc.). The uncut part of the block is the positive image and forms the printing surface. The most familiar relief printing techniques are: linoleum cut, woodcut, and wood engraving, but practically any material can be used. The early dotted print or crible is a surface print. The same, however, can also be intaglio printed. In contemporary printmaking we often see the combination of both printing methods. Any metal or even plastic plate incised or worked in relief can first be intaglio inked, then surface rolled, and then printed, thus combining both processes. To make a relief print one can also build up a surface with plastics, paper, cardboard, etc.

Relief printing generally lends itself best to a bold concept of design, more areas than lines. The early German woodcut is a *tour de force*, but even these are coarse compared with a metal engraving.

[34]

VASILI KANDINSKI, *Abstraction* (FROM "KLEINE WELTEN"). 1922. LITHOGRAPH, 10 $^{15}\!/_{16}$ X 9$^{1}\!/_{16}$. GIFT OF ABBY ALDRICH ROCKEFELLER, MUSEUM OF MODERN ART, NEW YORK.

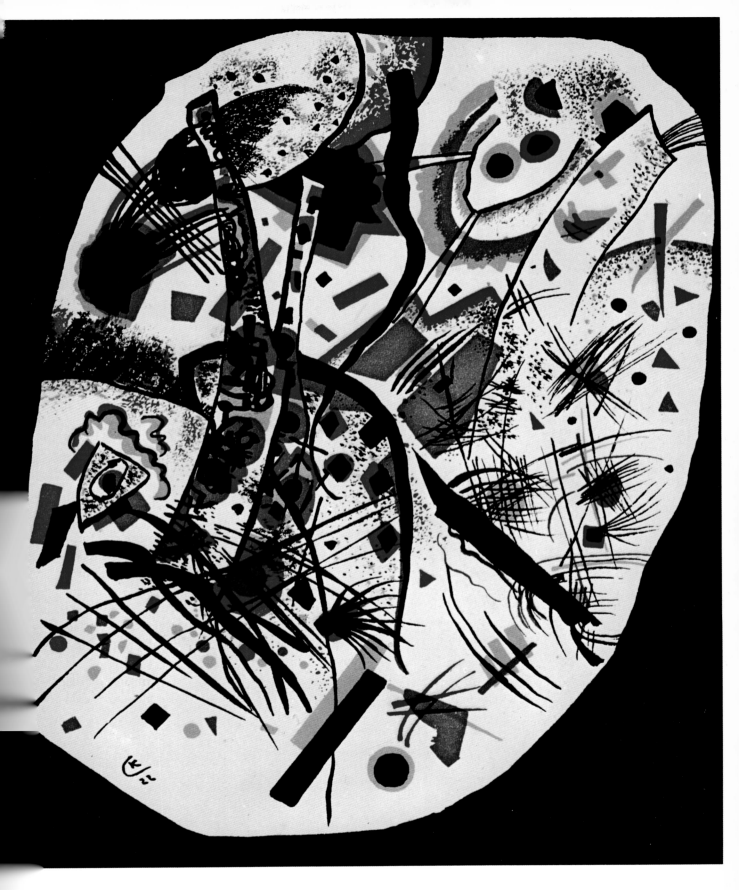

Illustration from *Encyclope de Recueil*, Intaglio print shop. Fig. A, inking of plate. Fig. B, hand-wiping the plate. Fig. C., printing. Paris, 1767. Burndy Library, Norwalk.

Incised Processes (INTAGLIO)

Intaglio printing is the opposite of relief printing. The design is cut, scratched, or etched into the printing surface or plate (copper, zinc, aluminum, magnesium, plastics, or even coated paper). It is printed from the incision, or grooves below the surface. The printing ink is rubbed into these areas and the surface is wiped clean.

While surface printing generally does not require much pressure, and woodcuts or linoleum cuts can be printed by rubbing the paper with a wooden spoon, intaglio printing requires great pressure. Intaglio printing is actually a process of embossing the paper into the incised lines. Many of the contemporary prints are made as pure embossments, without any inking of the lowered areas. The following are the major working methods for

[35]

ÉDOUARD VUILLARD, *La Cuisiniere*. LITHOGRAPH, 14⅛ x 10¾. BROOKLYN MUSEUM.

intaglio printing: line engraving, etching, drypoint, aquatint, mezzotint, stipple engraving, metal graphic, cellocut, collograph, etc. (For descriptions see glossary.)

Intaglio processes are probably the most versatile, as the various techniques can produce any effect, from the most delicate to the boldest.

Planographic Process (LITHOGRAPHY)

The planographic process involves printing from a flat surface. The method of lithography is based on the principle that water and oil don't mix. The image is drawn or painted on stone or especially granulated zinc, with a greasy crayon or tousch. After going through various steps of etch, the stone or plate is ready to print. Next, the printing surface is moistened. The greasy part of the stone rejects the water, the clean surface retains it. When this surface is rolled up with printing ink, the reverse happens. The wet part of the stone repels the ink, the greasy part attracts it.

Lithography lends itself to spontaneous, direct crayon or brush drawing. It is adaptable to rich tonal variations and to painterly color work. (More about the lithography method in the glossary.)

Stencil Processes

Stenciling, that is, applying color through the cut-out sections of paper or any other suitable material, is one of the oldest printing methods known. It has been used practically all over the world for decorative purposes, principally for textile printing. Silk screen is a more sophisticated contemporary variation of stencil printing. (More on silk-screen printing in glossary under Serigraph.)

Stencil methods are particularly suited to print flat or textured areas of color. They can be used in combination with the three other processes: intaglio, relief, or planographic.

Glossary of Graphic Terms
and Techniques

Aquatint

An intaglio method to etch tones or textures into a metal plate. The plate is dusted with powdered rosin (colophony). This can be done by hand, using a bag, or by placing the plate in a dust box. Next, the plate is heated to melt the rosin dust. The melted rosin adheres to the plate and forms a continuous but porous ground. The density and texture of the aquatint ground can be controlled by the dusting process. One can combine fine- and coarse-grain rosin, etc. Before etching, the aquatint design is controlled by "stopping out" (covering with varnish) the negative, nontonal, or white areas on the plate. The tonal values of aquatint are controlled by the length of the etching process. The longer you etch the deeper are the tones. The time element in the aquatint etch is more delicate than in line etching.

Aquatint can be combined with most of the intaglio methods, and is seldom used alone.

Outstanding examples are the works of Goya and Rouault.

Bite

The action of acids or corrosive agents on metal.

Bleeding

Oil seepage around a printed line or blotching of a printed line. The latter can be the result of ink that is too liquid, lines that are too deep, or too much printing pressure.

A. Woodcut. Surface printing. Bold contrasts. Solid and textured areas.
B. Dotted print. Surface printing. Tones are created with punched textures.
C. Line engraving on metal. Intaglio printing. Sharp, precise, swelling, and tapering lines.
D. Line etching. Intaglio printing. The variations in the lines and textures are controlled by the choices of metals, acids, and the length of the bite.

E. Drypoint. Intaglio printing. Scratched lines on metal. Fuzzy warm, velvety blacks. Hard to control and wears out easily.

F. Mezzotint. Intaglio printing. Rich blacks, and luminous passages achieved with burnishing and scraping a burr-covered metal surface.

G. Stipple engraving and etching. Intaglio printing. Mellow tonal passages achieved by either engraved or etched tiny dots.

H. Lithography. Planographic process. Granular lines and textures. Also flat areas, and sharp edges depending on the stone surface and drawing material.

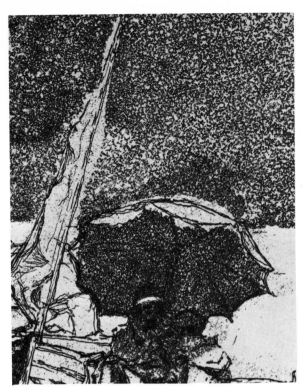

I. Aquatint etching. Intaglio printing. Granulous tonal areas simulating the effect of washes.

J. Sugar lift or liftground etching. A method of etching direct and spontaneous brush strokes with aquatint.

K. Wood engraving. Surface printing. Fine, delicate lines and textures cut into cross-grained wood blocks with gravers.

L. Soft ground etching. Intaglio printing. A method of etching textures into metal. It can be combined with other methods.

M. Linoleum cut. Surface printing. Similar to woodcut except the absence of wood grains makes it more mechanical.

N. Cellocut-Collography variety of new methods using plastics and glues combined with other materials to build a printing surface. They can be both surface and intaglio printed.

O. Metalgraphic. Intaglio printing. Building up a printing surface with various metals.

P. Silk screen print or serigraph. Stenciling method. Wide range from big bold areas to delicate textures. Primarily used for color.

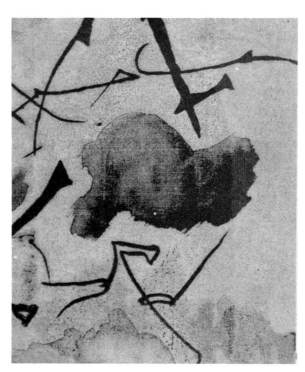

Cellocut

A method originated by Boris Margo. A surface, design, or texture built up with liquid plastics on a support—wood, metal, cardboard, or plastic. When solidified, this surface can be further altered with the use of various cutting and scraping tools. It can be printed both as an intaglio or relief process, and combined with other media.

Chiaroscuro Woodcut

Developed in the early sixteenth century. First printed color woodcuts in Europe. Simulated drawings on colored paper with touched-up white highlights. It involves two or more separate printing blocks. One, the key block, generally printed in black or any dark color for the details, and the other blocks with the highlights cut out for the tones. Outstanding practitioners were Hans Burckmair, Lucas Cranach, Hans Grien Baldung.

Cliche Verre

This method of duplication was used by a few artists in the nineteenth century. The idea came from the principle of photography, although Cliche Verre prints did not have the tonal variations of a photograph. The artist first covered a piece of clear glass with an opaque pigment or emulsion, then scratched with a sharp stylus through this protective coating. When the drawing was finished, the glass plate (negative) was placed on photo-sensitized paper, exposed to light, and developed. The result was a (positive) print in strong black and white contrast. Of all the artists who experimented with this method, Corot was the most important.

Collector's Mark

See chapter on collecting.

Collograph

This is a fairly recent method of building up a printing surface. The printing plate is created by gluing all kinds of textures (sawdust, wood shavings, ground walnut shells, wrinkled paper, sand, etc.) to a support, such as cardboard, masonite, etc. The textures have to be imbedded into a tough, and nonabsorbent adhesive like Elmer's Glue, Lucite, or Epoxy. The plate can be printed in intaglio or relief.

Counter Proof

After a plate or wood block is printed, a clean sheet of paper is placed on the wet proof and run through the press or rubbed by hand. The resulting offset image from the wet print onto the second paper is the counter proof. As the first print is a reverse image of the plate, the counter proof is reversed back to the same direction as the plate. This is very useful for the artist as it is easier to read than a reverse image when corrections are made on a plate.

Creeping Bite

To etch in stages by the gradual submersion of the plate in the acid. Generally used with aquatint when a subtle transition of tone is desired.

Crible or Dotted Print

A dotted print is made by punching hollows and making incisions into the metal plate. Generally printed on relief, the design appears as white dots on a black background. These are the earliest European metal prints.

Double Run

To run a plate through the press twice in order to get a heavier impression.

Dropping Out

To cut out, to scrape out, to dig out, to eliminate out of the printing plate or wood block.

Drypoint

This is an intaglio method of creating a design by scratching lines into metal plates (copper, zinc, soft steel, etc.) with hard steel or diamond-point needles. In the drypoint technique the incision into the plate is negligible, it is the metal burr raised by the steel or diamond point that holds the ink. As the burr is rugged and irregular it prints as a soft velvety line, the opposite of the sharp precise engraved line.

Master of the Clubs, Calvary. Dotted print, 7⅛ x 4⅝. Rosenwald Collection, National Gallery of Art, Washington, D.C.

Drypoints are delicate to print as the burrs are easily flattened down by the printing pressure. Thus, unless the artist is satisfied with a very limited number of proofs (three) or four unless the plate is continually retouched like Rembrandt's), the plate has to be steel-faced. This is a process of depositing hard iron by electrolytic means on the copper plate. This coating is very thin and if it is properly done, it hardens the burrs without considerable effect on its printing quality. Outstanding examples of drypoint were produced by the Master of the Amsterdam Cabinet, Rembrandt, Whistler, Corinth, and Beckman.

Embossed Print (GAUFFRAGE, BLINDPRESSING)

Pressing the paper into the lowered areas of the plate or wood block, thus creating a three-dimensional, sculptural effect. All intaglio prints are embossed but in this case the lowered or incised areas are uninked. Embossment can be achieved with handrubbing like on some Japanese woodcuts or on an etching press using heavy dampened rag paper. At the present there is such a great interest in the sculptural print that one might call it a fad. Some younger artists are working with such a deep relief that special presses have had to be constructed to print them. Michael Ponce de Leon has a hydraulic press built by Charles Brandt that can exert over ten thousand pounds of pressure to the square inch.

Engraving, Line (GRAVURE SUR CUIVRE, KUPFERSTICH)

To engrave is to cut the design into metal with a graver or burin. Although it was known long before as a method to decorate metal surfaces, it appeared as a printing method only during the first half of the fifteenth century. The burin or graver is a lozenge-shaped steel rod with a slightly bent shank. The cutting is done by pushing the burin into the metal plate. The deeper it penetrates into the metal, the wider is the line. This creates the swelling-tapering character, or the engraved line. After the engraving is finished the slight burr raised by the graver is cleaned off with a scraper. The engraved line is sharp and clean, the opposite of drypoint. It is a very intense line that would assert itself even if cut over a densely etched area. Today, there are very few pure engravings made. Outstanding masters of engraving are: Mantegna, Schongauer, Dürer, and Duvet.

Etching (EAU FORTE, RADIERUNG)

A design is worked into the metal by the corrosive action of acids. The plate is first covered with a uniform coat of ground (acid resistant coating). This can be rolled on the

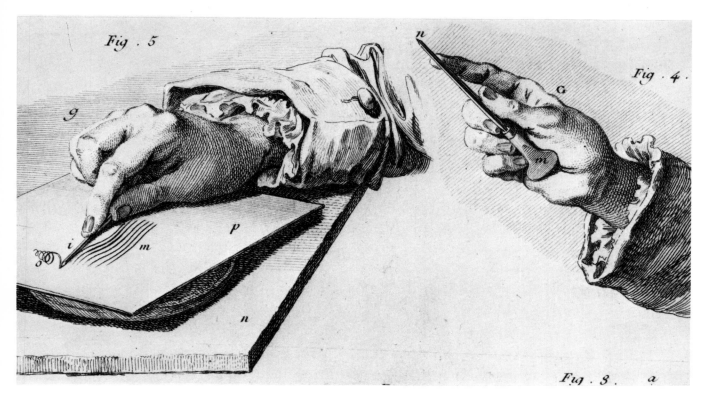

Illustration from *Encyclope de Recueil*, Metal engraving. Paris, 1767. Burndy Library, Norwalk.

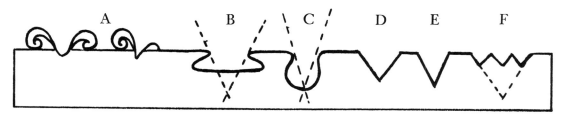

A. Drypoint lines showing variety of burrs.
B. Shallow line with strong undercut etched with nitric acid.
C. Line etched with Dutch mordant on copper.
D. Engraved line with standard square graver.
E. Engraved line with lozenge shaped graver.
F. Wide lines are engraved with touching parallel cuts.

[46]

heated plate or brushed on. After the ground solidifies (hard ground) the artist can start working on it with various pointed metal tools (etching needle, pen points, electric drill, razor blade, etc.). Where the ground is removed, the metal is exposed to the action of the acid. The etched line is generally a fairly even threadlike line of uniform thickness (no swelling or tapering like in engraving) but its character can vary greatly depending on the choice of the metal and the type of acid used. For controlled, regular bite, it is best to use Dutch mordant on copper. For rugged, irregular bite use nitric acid on zinc plate. The character of the bite is further controlled by the strength of the acid solution. The depth and the thickness is controlled by the length of the bite. A plate can be etched in stages by covering some of the already etched areas with stop out varnish and etching the rest longer. This procedure can be repeated many times. Most artists develop their plates by re-etching them many times. After each state the ground is removed, the plate printed, then the whole process repeated as many times as is necessary. This procedure is partially responsible for the richness of color in Rembrandt's plates.

Soft Ground Etching

Soft ground is basically the same acid resistant coating as the hard ground except that it contains approximately one-third grease. The grease keeps the ground in semi-hard or tacky condition, thus it can be used to take impressions of various textures (textiles, crumpled paper, leaves, etc.) The textures are placed on the soft ground covered plate and run through on the press. The design is controlled by stopping out areas that we don't want to etch. Then the remaining textures are etched into the metal the same way as the conventional hard ground etching. This technique lends itself well to collage type effects on the plate.

Initially, in the nineteenth century, soft ground was used for a different effect. The artist placed a paper on the grounded plate and made his drawing on the paper with a pencil or any other drawing instrument. The paper picked up the soft ground under the pressure of the drawing instrument and produced a soft granulous line, resembling a litho crayon drawing. This was then etched the same way as the others.

Lift Ground Etching (*sugar-lift aquatint*)

The main principle is to etch a positive image on aquatint by drawing with a water soluble ground. With the conventional aquatint technique the artist controls the image by stopping out the negative areas with varnish; he has to work around the positive image. With lift ground, a wash-out principle, he uses a viscous liquid (India ink, Gamboge, or ordinary poster paint mixed with sugar syrup, glycerin, etc.) to paint on the plate. After the painting is finished and dried, the whole thing is covered with thin liquid hard ground. After the ground dries the plate can be placed into lukewarm water that dissolves, lifts the design, and exposes the plate to the acid. The aquatinting can be handled two ways, according to preference. Either the whole plate can be aquatinted before painting with lift ground, or it can be aquatinted after the design is lifted. The etching process is the same as aquatint biting. Picasso made some outstanding lift-ground etchings.

Relief Etching

Whole areas of the plate are etched down so that the unetched parts stand up in relief. Generally, this is done by painting the high areas with asphaltum varnish or liquid hard ground, then etching the plate in a strong acid solution. This process also can be done in stages to achieve different levels. This is particularly important in color printing, where the various levels can carry different colors applied with rollers of varying density. Most of the recent sculptural prints are made with relief etching.

Etching Ground

Acid resistant coating applied on metal plates. The design is scratched into the ground, then etched. Regular hard ground generally consists of two parts of asphaltum, two parts of bee's wax, and one part of rosin.

Feathering

To remove or stir with a feather or brush the bubbles produced by the action of nitric acid on zinc or copper plates.

Foul Bite

Accidental etching of an area.

Intaglio Color Plate

To overprint several color intaglio plates on the same paper.

Intaglio Mixed Methods

This is the combination of several intaglio methods on the same plate. Many etchings are in this category. Goya mixed line etching and aquatint, Rembrandt mixed line etching and drypoint, for example.

Intaglio Printing

Printing from the crevices and grooves engraved or etched into the plate. A fairly stiff printing ink is rubbed into the lines, then the surface of the plate is wiped with a rag (tarlatan) and might be finished with a handwipe. Printing an intaglio print is more delicate than relief printing as the inking and wiping process can vary much more. The tones and the richness of the lines are affected by the printing ink, paper quality, type of wipe, and pressure of the press.

Intaglio prints are made on damp, preferably pure rag paper. As the paper has to be embossed into the incisions, the paper fibers have to be soft.

Intaglio printing is made on an etching press. This is a simple but sturdy machine, consisting of a steel press bed traveling between two steel rollers. Most presses are equipped with a very rudimentary screw type pressure adjustment.

The actual printing process of an intaglio plate is as follows: The inked and wiped plate is placed face up on the press bed. The damp printing paper is placed on the plate. The paper is covered with several layers of woven wool felts (this resilient cover helps the embossing), then the press bed is driven through between the steel rollers. A good intaglio print needs evenly distributed heavy pressure. But even that can vary according to the character of the point or the technique used. For instance, a drypoint has to be printed with much less pressure than a line engraving.

Key Plate or Block

The plate or block used to serve as a guide to register other plates or blocks in color printing.

Lift Ground

See Etching.

Linoleum Cut

One of the simplest and most direct relief printing processes. It is used a great deal to introduce children to printmaking. The negative parts of the design are cut out with knives or gauges. Printing ink is rolled on the raised surface of the design. It can be printed by hand rubbing, or mounted on type high wood block on a letter press or screw press. Matisse and Picasso made outstanding lino-cuts.

Lithography (PLANOGRAPHIC PROCESS)

Invented by Aloys Senefelder in 1798. This method is based on the principle that water and grease do not mix. The image is drawn or painted on the stone or zinc plate with greasy litho crayon or ink (tousch). Once the drawing is finished it has to be fixed with an etch to prevent the spreading of the grease. The term "etch" is rather confusing because most people immediately identify it with metal etching where the result is a drastic alteration of the printing surface. In lithography the etch is a syrupy mixture of gum arabic mixed with a small quantity of nitric acid. This is used basically to protect the drawing from water and to further desensitize the undrawn areas to printing ink.

After the stone is properly etched and thus the design fixed, it can be washed out with turpentine. Now all the visible aspects of the design disappears, but it is locked into the stone by the grease. After the cleaned stone dries, it can be wetted with a sponge and rolled up with litho-ink. The ungreasy areas of the stone retain the water and reject the printing ink. The greasy parts attract the ink, thus the image reappears. It is ready now to be proved or printed on a dampened, fairly smooth rag paper.

The litho press consists of a steel bed traveling under a leather-faced scraper. The scraper exerts the printing pressure and can be adjusted.

Lithography lends itself well to a great range of drawing techniques. Tones can be achieved by rubbing soft crayons, or by washes and dry brush. Scratch techniques are made with needles, razor blades, and sandpaper. Textures can also be spluttered or transferred from various materials with an offset technique. Lithography is well suited for color printing. Outstanding examples: Toulouse-Lautrec, Bonnard, Vuillard, Munch, Picasso.

Mezzotint (MANIER NOIR)

An intaglio method of creating a dark surface by roughing up the plate with a tool called a "rocker" and working back toward the light tones with scraping and burnishing. Mezzotint, like drypoint, holds the ink by the burrs created on the surface. This produces a rich velvety quality, but fragile print. Mezzotint is primarily a tonal process and therefore is ideally suited to reproduce paintings. However, the creative work produced in this media is negligible.

Monotype or Monoprint

A print in an edition of one; a unique print. Actually it is a printed painting or printed drawing. The artist can paint on various surfaces such as metal, plastic, and glass, and

HENRI MATISSE, *Desting* (FROM "THE JAZZ SERIES"). 1947. SERIGRAPH, 16¼ X 25. GIFT OF THE ARTIST, MUSEUM OF MODERN ART, NEW YORK.

53/80   Miró. 1952

then print it either by rubbing or on an etching press. The primary value of monotypes is that in offsetting the image from the plate to the paper it achieves a quality and luminosity of its own. Degas made some remarkable monotypes, both figures and landscapes. I have experimented extensively with an offset monotype technique.

Mixed Media

To work with a combination of techniques on the same print.

Offset Printing or Offsetting

Indirect printing, by depositing an image from one roller or plate to another and then printing it on the paper.

Paper, Printing Papers

The development of papermaking had an important role in the history of printmaking. No invention had greater influence on human culture than paper, yet most people know so little about it. Certainly everybody interested in the graphic arts should have at least a superficial knowledge of its history and manufacture. The word "paper" itself is the source of a great deal of confusion. It is derived from the Latin "papyrus," therefore, most people think that this was an early form of paper, a mistaken notion.

Papyrus was made from the pith of a sedge growing in abundance in the Nile valley. The Egyptians and other Mediterranean people used it as a writing substance. The manufacture of papyrus is made by laminating strips of the sedge pith. Paper is made by macerating fibers to form a watery solution of pulp.

There is also a great deal of confusion with the term "rice paper." This inaccurate term is generally identified with most papers made in the Orient. The so-called "rice paper" is made of the pith of a plant growing in Formosa. This sheer, white substance, used to make artificial flowers, is neither a paper, nor is it made of rice. Rice cannot be used to make paper.

Papermaking was invented in China, approximately in the second century A.D. The system was amazingly simple. Leftover silk strips were soaked in water and beat until they became a fibrous pulp. This pulp was then spread evenly on a screen (mold) to allow drainage for the excess water. Dried, the thin layer of fibrous pulp became paper. It is worth noting that the basic principle of handmade paper is still the same all over the world.

[51]

JOAN MIRÓ, *Le chien aboyant a la Lune* (FROM *Verve*). LITHOGRAPH, 14¼ x 21⅜. LARRY ALD-RICH FUND, MUSEUM OF MODERN ART, NEW YORK.

The mechanics of the mold was improved, the preparation of the pulp became more efficient, but the fundamental process remained the same.

The most primitive method of pouring the pulp on a stretched woven grass screen is still practiced in some areas in the Orient. The more sophisticated method is to dip the mold into a pulp-filled vat, shake it for even distribution, and dry it. The modern paper mill is a mechanized application of these principles.

It is fascinating to follow paper's long journey from China to the West.

A.D.	105	Paper invented in Lei-yang
A.D.	610	Paper introduced to Japan from Korea
A.D.	751	Paper made in Samarkand
A.D.	793	Paper is introduced in Bagdad
A.D.	900	Paper is made in Egypt
A.D.	1100	Morocco learns papermaking from Egypt
A.D.	1151	First paper mill at Xativa, Spain
A.D.	1276	Paper manufacturing begins at Fabriano, Italy. This paper mill is still in existence.
A.D.	1348	Paper mill in Troyes, France
A.D.	1390	Paper mill started in Nuremberg, Germany
A.D.	1657	First English paper mill in Hertfordshire
A.D.	1690	First American paper mill in Germantown, Pennsylvania

In Japan, paper is made of vegetable fibers. Kozo, gampi, and mitsumata are the three most commonly used plants for this purpose. The most popular mulberry paper is made of kozo. In the Orient, the preparation of the vegetable fibers is considered the most important step in papermaking. Most oriental craftsmen still prefer to do it by hand in order to produce fibers of the correct length.

The West used linen and cotton rags instead of raw vegetable fibers as its basic material for paper. The water-soaked rags were rolled into large balls and fermented for weeks. When fungi appeared on the surface of the balls it was a sign that the rags were ready for making the paper. Some experts think that the "foxing" of old papers is due to excessive fermenting in the manufacturing process.

The distinction between various types of paper often relates to the mold construction. The mold is a wooden frame inside of which a wire screen is stretched. The "chain" lines run up and down the short dimensions of the paper, one-half to two inches apart. The "laid" lines run the long way, twenty to forty to the inch.

The deckle is a removable wooden frame that is placed inside of the mold to determine the size of the paper. Therefore, deckled paper is associated with handmade paper. The definition of "laid" or "woven" paper refers to the screen impression on the paper and has nothing to do with its manufacturing. Woven paper doesn't exist.

Pressing and sizing are the last important steps in papermaking, as they determine the surface characteristics. The more pressure exerted on the paper the harder is its surface. For instance, water-color papers come in cold pressed or hot pressed variety; the hot pressed is the harder. The last step is the sizing. This is the application of a thin layer of glue or gelatin. The quantity of sizing will determine the absorbing qualities of the paper; without sizing, all papers would be as absorbent as blotting paper. For printmakers the amount of sizing in the paper is critical as it determines how long the paper has to be soaked before it prints well.

Papermaking became such a big industry in the West that eventually a shortage of rags developed. All kinds of laws and regulations were enacted in Europe as well as in America to conserve the raw materials essential to papermaking. In England a law was passed forbidding the burial of anyone in clothing usable for the manufacture of paper.

From the eighteenth century on, there was continuous experimentation to replace rags as the sole source of papermaking. The big turning point came at the end of the eighteenth century in England when Matthias Koops started to manufacture paper in large quantities made of wood pulp. From that point on wood-pulp papers gradually replaced rag papers in commercial use. Wood paper was cheap and its raw material was plentiful. Unfortunately, this paper is not durable and in time becomes brittle. It also has a tendency to yellow with age. Another disadvantage of wood-pulp paper has to do with its manufacture. In order to reproduce a white paper, strong chemical bleaches, sulfites, have to be used. So far no way has been found to remove all traces of these chemicals. Thus, on extended contact, the remainder of sulfuric acid in the pulp paper stains and burns other materials. These are the reasons why this type of paper is not suitable for fine art work, and why it is so dangerous to mount fine prints with cheap cardboards.

Parchment

The inner side of sheepskin, separated from the outside. After special treatment of its surface it was used for writing. In Europe it was in wide use before the introduction of paper manufacture. After that it was used mostly for important documents.

Planographic Process

See Lithography.

Pl. X.

Papetterie, Cuve à Ouvrer.

Illustration from *Encyclope de Recueil*, Papermaking. Paris, 1767. Burndy Library, Norwalk.

Glossary of Graphic Terms and Techniques

Plaster Print

It can be either a print made by casting plaster on an inked intaglio plate, or a relief print made from an inked plaster plate.

Printing a La Poupe

A color printing method developed in France. Instead of using separate plates for the various colors, the different color areas are individually inked and wiped on the same plate. The inking is made with a specially folded pointed tarlatan "poupe." This is a rather tedious process, admirably controlled by expert Parisian printers.

Process Prints (PHOTOMECHANICAL METHODS OF REPRODUCTIONS)

Process print is a collective name for all photomechanically produced prints. In this book we are only indirectly concerned with commercial printing methods. There is so much confusion and controversy about the original print concept that some knowledge of process printing is a must. I have to emphasize that the following descriptions are over-simplifications by necessity. A thorough description of all commercial printing methods could be the subject of a large book in itself. There are, however, many manuals treating those subjects in depth for anybody interested in more information than I can give within the limitation of this book.

LINE CUT OR LINE BLOCK

Line cut is the simplest and cheapest of all the photoreproductive processes. It is used only to reproduce straight black and white drawings, as it cannot register tonalities. If tones are needed in a line cut they can be achieved with the use of Ben Day screens (textures made out of dots). Most newspaper advertising uses this inexpensive method.

The basic principle of line cut is similar to woodcut and it can be used to reproduce them. I have seen this type of reproduction printed on good paper, and sold as an original woodcut.

Line cuts are made on photoengravers zinc plate or on a similar metal alloy (zome, micrometal, aluminum, magnesium) coated with an emulsion of albumin or gelatin mixed with potassium bichromate. This emulsion hardens on exposure to light. The light passing through the transparent parts of the negative (the dark areas on the positive image) hardens the albumin emulsion. The protected emulsion areas by the blacks of the negative remain in their soluable state.

The plate is then rolled over the greasy ink and soaked in water. The unexposed, soft emulsion is washed out by the water. After the plate is dried it is dusted with powdered rosin that adheres to the remaining inked emulsion areas. The plate is then heated to melt the rosin. This forms an acid-resistant coating. This procedure is similar to the aquatint used by artists. The plate is then etched long enough to make the positive part of the image stand up in high relief. This is important because if the white or negative areas touch the printing paper it might produce a blurred, fuzzy print.

HALF-TONE CUT OR BLOCK

Half-tone cut is a more sophisticated method than line cut, capable of reproducing fine tonal variations. The basic principle is to fragment tonal areas into tiny dots of various sizes. When printed, these create the optical illusion of continuous tones and textures. First, the subject to be reproduced is photographed through a glass screen. This screen consists of fine lines printed on glass at right angles. This creates thousands of tiny openings through which the subject is photographed. The result is an image broken up into dots corresponding to the openings on the screen. There are great variations in screens from coarse (50 lines per inch) to the finest (175 lines per inch). The selection of the screen is dictated by the paper to be used for printing. For newsprint paper a coarse screen is used, but the fine screens must be printed on a hard, coated paper.

After the photo negative of the image is finished, it is printed on a sensitized copper plate. (For half tone, cut copper is much better than zinc because the fine details need a more controlled etch.) From that point on the procedure of wash out and etch is similar to the one used on the line cut.

Half-tone cut prints can be readily recognized by the regular screen pattern. The coarse 50-line screen can be seen with the naked eye, but finer screens should be examined with a magnifying glass.

Both the line cut and the half-tone cut are mounted type high on a wood block. This is necessary as these plates are usually printed in combination with type, and the presses are adjusted to that standard height.

HALF-TONE COLOR REPRODUCTION

This is a rather complex and expensive process. First a color separation is made by photographing the original to be reproduced through a series of color filters. A half-tone plate has to be made for each color to be used. Generally four colors are used: the three basic colors, red, yellow, blue; and black. Fine photoengraving houses specializing in art reproductions often use many more color plates. When all the plates are finished, they are overprinted. The individual plates are made the same way as a regular black and white half-tone cut, but usually the color plates have to be worked over by hand to establish the proper balance between them. The slightest inaccuracy in any of the color plates can ruin all the colors. It is also very important to print these plates in perfect register as off register would create fuzzy moire patterns.

ROTOGRAVURE

In the rotogravure process a thin copper plate is attached to a cylinder, functioning in a web-fed rotary press. To make the plate a reversed half-tone screen is used with a grid of transparent lines and opaque black squares. On exposure to light, the emulsion on the plate hardens under the lines but leaves the squares soft. Then the same plate is exposed again through a diapositive (a photographic positive of the subject). This time the soft emulsion squares harden in proportion to the range of grays. In etching this plate the softest squares are affected by the acid first, and the hardest ones the last. The result after the etch is a plate covered with squares of equal sizes but various depths. As the deep squares hold more ink than the shallow ones, the tonalities in the reproduction are controlled in the same manner as in all intaglio printing methods. The rotogravure plate is inked by rotating against another ink-carrying cylinder, and wiped by a steel blade that removes all excess ink from its surface with a scraping action. As the grid on a rotogravure plate is raised it appears as white lines on the print. It can easily be identified by this characteristic.

Although rotogravure is an intaglio printing process, it uses dry paper, light pressure, and thin ink. Therefore, it has hardly any embossment.

PHOTOLITHOGRAPHIC OFFSET

Lithographic method applied to commercial mass production. As the photo offset plate has to be mounted on a cylinder, instead of stone, specially treated thin zinc or aluminum plates are used. The image is photographed on the sensitized litho plate through a screen. The offset method is double printing. The image from the zinc plate is printed on another roller covered with a rubber blanket. From the rubber the image is printed on the paper. As the image is twice reversed, the final print corresponds to the original plate. As the litho offset ink is too thin to speed up the inking and facilitate transfer, the tonal areas lose some of their richness and tend to print gray. Litho offset can be used also for color printing. The color separation follows the same principle as with the half-tone color plate. This method is often used to forge original lithographs. Printed on a rich paper it can easily deceive the layman, so it is always advisable to examine prints with a magnifying glass.

Proof Before Letters

Many old prints, particularly seventeenth- and eighteenth-century reproductive prints carried engraved information on the lower margin. Usually this consisted of the engraver's name, the designing artist, the publisher's name, the title of the print, and the publishing date. Often it also included an elaborate dedication to a patron. The text was usually engraved on the plate by a professional letter engraver after the image was finished. Publishers usually printed a limited number of proofs before the lettering was added to the plate, and sold them at premium prices. This was based on the often erroneous concept that the early proofs are always better than the late ones. In this case it was justified only with drypoints, and mezzotints made before the invention of steel-facing.

Relief Etching

See Etching.

Relief Printing

To print from the design surface standing on relief. Color is generally applied with rollers and printing can be made with either rubbing pressure, scraping pressure, straight pressure, or rolling pressure. The same principle applies to process printing also, except that it is accomplished mechanically.

Rollers or Brayers

They can be made of rubber, gelatin, and plastic of different sizes and densities. They are used to roll printing ink on plates, stones, and wood blocks.

Repoussage

To press or hammer back a low area on the plate created either by excessive etching or by scraping on its original level.

Retroussage

To pull the ink out of the lines lightly with muslin, of an otherwise cleanly wiped plate, in order to make a richer print.

Serigraphy or Silk Screen

Serigraphy is the name given to the silk screen by artists to get away from its commercial associations. Silk screen is a sophisticated stencil process, developed around the beginning of the nineteenth century and first used mostly for commercial advertising and display work. Fine artists started to use it extensively during the last fifteen to twenty years. Most recently, artists like Rauschenberg and Warhol have used silk-screen printing on canvas as part of their painting process.

The process got its name from the fine mesh silk tacked to a wooden frame to serve as a support for an intricately cut paper stencil. The printing was based on the simple principle that the open mesh of the silk lets the paint through, while the paper stencils glued to it blocks it out. Later on, the method became more and more sophisticated. The silk was replaced with more durable metal screens (copper, aluminum, and plastic) and the paper stencil was replaced with more flexible and versatile materials. Artists started to use the tousche and crayon method, simulating the lift-ground etching principle. The design was painted or drawn on the screen with lithographic tousch or crayon, then the whole screen was covered with a light coat of glue. After the glue dried the screen was washed out with benzine or kerosene. These solvents removed the tousch or crayon but didn't dissolve the glue. Thus the paint could penetrate the open mesh under the design.

The latest development in silk-screen printing is the introduction of photosensitized film as stencil. This allows the designer to use photographic reproductions of a drawing or even the reproduction of photographs. The sale of these as original prints creates a great deal of controversy and it is more thoroughly discussed in the chapter on original prints.

To print silk screen, the wooden frame holding the screen is hinged to a slightly larger wood board. The printing paper is placed on the board, under the screen. The printing ink is pressed through the screen by hand with a squeegee (a rubber blade set in a wooden handle, usually the same width as the screen). Any number of colors can be used, a separate screen for each color.

Soft Ground

See Etching.

Steel-Facing

To deposit a thin layer of steel by galvanic process on the surface of a copper plate to make it more resistant to wear. See drypoint.

Stipple Print

Stipple etching and engraving is to create a half-tone effect by either etching or engraving tiny dots into the plate.

Sugar Lift

See Lift Ground Etching under Etching.

Surface Print

The color or printing ink deposited on the surface of the metal plate or wood block and printed by rubbing, by straight or rolling pressure.

Undercut

The formulation of a cavity created by the side-biting tendency of acids. This is often the cause of a "creve," the crumbling of densely textured areas on the plate by over-etching. Rembrandt often retouched these areas with drypoint.

Vellum

The whole calf skin treated with lime and used for writing. "Vellum" is the misleading name of a paper resembling parchment.

Watermarks

Identification mark of the manufacturer embossed into the paper. The watermark is made by sawing an emblem made out of twisted wire onto the paper mold. Watermarks are important factors in determining the authenticity of old prints. Briquet's *Dictionary of Watermarks* (Geneva) is the best reference book on this subject.

Woodcut (GRAVURE SUR BOIS, HOLZSCHNITT)

The earliest relief printing method. In the East, eighth century, in the West, early fifteenth.

The design is either painted directly onto the wood block or pasted on it. The cutter (either the artist himself or a skilled craftsman) cuts all the surface away except the design.

The depth of the relief depends on how open the design is, but generally it varies between one-eighth to one-quarter inch depth.

Woodcut is made on wood blocks (pear, rose, pine, apple, beech) cut plankwise. A special knife is used for fine lines and to cut textures. To clear larger areas, gauges of various shapes and sizes are used. In cutting, the grain of the wood has to be considered as it is more difficult to cut a clean line cross-grain than parallel with it. If the tool is not as sharp as a razor, it tears the wood cross-grain.

The traditional and contemporary concept of cutting is totally different. In traditional cutting, the cutter follows a design slavishly, while in contemporary concept the cutting itself is an integral part of the designing process.

For the printing of woodcuts see Relief Printing.

Outstanding examples of traditional woodcuts are the works of Dürer, for the modern concept those of Gauguin.

Wood Engraving (GRAVURE SUR BOIT DEBOUT. HOLZSTICH)

Wood engraving is a variation of woodcut. The preparation of the wood block creates the main difference between the two methods. While for woodcut the wood is cut plankwise, for wood engraving it is cut cross-grain. This eliminates the problem of grains. The cutter can move freely in any direction and instead of the large gauges he can use gravers and fine gauges. The principle of wood engraving is very close to the early sixteenth-century dotted print. In both the image is created by fine white lines and textures.

Wood engraving is an eighteenth-century English invention. It was used mostly for book illustrations and for reproductions. Thomas Bevick is credited with the perfectioning of the media.

Great Prints of the World

ANTONIO POLLAIUOLO, *Battle of the Naked Men*. ENGRAVING, 16⅜ x 24. YALE UNIVERSITY
ART GALLERY, NEW HAVEN.

Antonio Pollaiuolo

1429–98, ITALIAN

Pollaiuolo was a Florentine painter, sculptor, architect, goldsmith, and one of the greatest engravers of the fifteenth century. He studied with Finiguerra, the founder of the Florentine school of engraving. Strangely enough, his reputation as a printmaker is based on two versions of the same subject: "The Battle of the Naked Man." This is a powerful image, beautifully engraved in the Florentine broad manner. It has a shallow space like a bas-relief indicating the goldsmith influence in his training, but this is compensated by the surface tension created by the rhythmic interplay between the struggling naked figures.

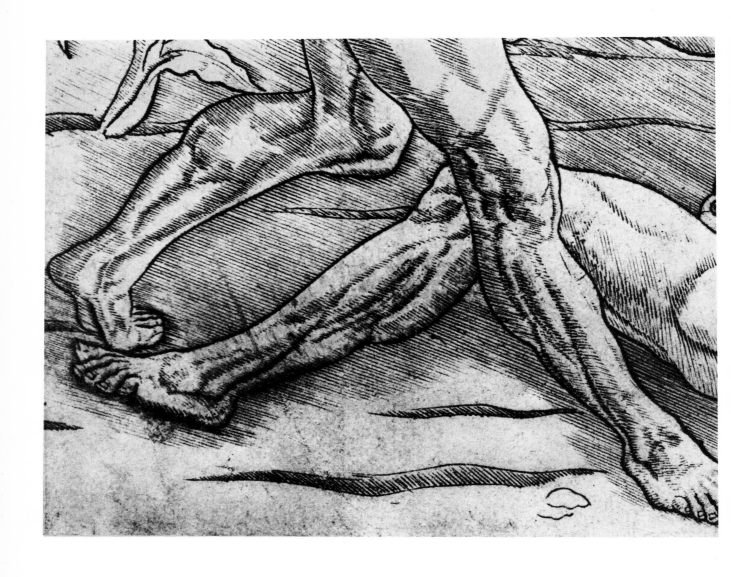

ANTONIO POLLAIUOLO, *Battle of the Naked Men*. ENGRAVING, DETAIL. YALE UNIVERSITY
ART GALLERY, NEW HAVEN.

Andrea Mantegna

1431–1506, ITALIAN

Mantegna was probably the finest printmaker Italy ever produced. He made approximately twenty plates, all of them line engravings. Some of his plates were lost. At the present, only seven of his prints are accepted by the experts as authentic. He had many followers, but none of them are considered outstanding artists.

ANDREA MANTEGNA, *Risen Christ.* ENGRAVING, 12½ x 11⅜. ROGERS FUND, METROPOLITAN MUSEUM OF ART, NEW YORK.

ANDREA MANTEGNA, *The Madonna and Child*. ENGRAVING, 8⅞ x 8⅝. ROSENWALD COLLECTION, NATIONAL GALLERY OF ART, WASHINGTON, D.C.

ANDREA MANTEGNA, *Roman Soldiers Bearing the Trophies in Triumph*. ENGRAVING. LIBRARY
OF CONGRESS, WASHINGTON, D.C.

Jacopo de' Barbari

c. 1440–c. 1516, ITALIAN

Painter, engraver, Barbari was born and died in Venice. He traveled
a great deal in Germany. In 1500 he was in Nuremberg working for
Maximilian. In 1507 he was in the Lowlands working for Phillip de
Bourgogne. He knew Dürer well; they traveled together and influenced each other. Dürer used some of Barbari's figure drawings in
his research on the proportions of the human body. Barbari learned
a great deal from the prints of Dürer. This is apparent in the engraving "Pegasus" reproduced in this book. Nevertheless, the peculiar
mixture of monumentality, grace, and delicacy of this print is his
very personal expression.

JACOPO de' BARBARI, *Pegasus.* ENGRAVING, 6 x 9. RIJKSMUSEUM, AMSTERDAM.

Master E. S.

FLOURISHED BETWEEN 1440–1467, GERMAN

One of the great men of medieval German art, we don't know much about Master E. S., yet he emerges from approximately 217 plates as a very strong and distinct personality. Although it is evident from his prints that, like most early engravers, he was first trained as a goldsmith, his work has a strong pictorial quality.

Master E. S. was one of the first to use initials as a signature on his plates, representing a transition from the complete anonymity of the Middle Ages to the more personalized attitude of the Renaissance. He used his initials as a goldsmith's hallmark, a guarantee of honest craftsmanship and a protection against imitators. This did not keep van Meckenem from retouching his plates and printing them with his own mark.

MASTER E. S., *Knight and Lady*. ENGRAVING, 5 1/32 X 3 3/32. HARRIS BRISBANE DICK FUND, METROPOLITAN MUSEUM OF ART, NEW YORK.

MASTER E. S., *Emperor Augustus and the Sibyl*. ENGRAVING, KATHERINE BULLARD FUND, MUSEUM OF FINE ARTS, BOSTON.

MASTER E. S., *St. John on the Isle of Patmos*. ENGRAVING, 8¼ x 5¾. GIFT OF MR. & MRS. POTTER
PALMER, ART INSTITUTE OF CHICAGO.

MASTER E. S., *St. John the Evangelist in the Wilderness*. ENGRAVING. MARIA ANTOINETTE EVANS
FUND, MUSEUM OF FINE ARTS, BOSTON.

Master of the Amsterdam Cabinet
(Master of Hausbuch)

WORKED BETWEEN 1467–1507

The Master of Hausbuch was one of the most interesting and enigmatic figures of fifteenth-century printmaking. His prints are extremely rare mainly because he used drypoint which in itself limited the number of prints he could pull from these plates. This gave rise to the theory that these plates were not made for the "professional" trade.

The Master of Hausbuch was a truly fine artist. His prints are vigorous, spontaneously drawn, and versatile in concept. He made approximately ninety plates with a wide range of moods, from high drama to delightfully comic. The only comprehensive collection of his work is in the print cabinet of the Rijksmuseum in Amsterdam. As this great artist is still relatively unknown I decided to include a representative selection of his prints.

MASTER OF THE AMSTERDAM CABINET, *Christ Helped by Angels*. DRYPOINT, 3 x 4¼.
RIJKSMUSEUM, AMSTERDAM.

MASTER OF THE AMSTERDAM CABINET, *St. Martin.* DRYPOINT, 5¼ x 7¾. RIJKS-
MUSEUM, AMSTERDAM.

MASTER OF THE AMSTERDAM CABINET, *The Bearing of the Cross*. DRYPOINT, 5⅛ x 7⅝.
RIJKSMUSEUM, AMSTERDAM.

MASTER OF THE AMSTERDAM CABINET, *Dog*. DRYPOINT, 5 X 5. RIJKSMUSEUM, AM-
STERDAM.

MASTER OF THE AMSTERDAM CABINET, *The Hunt*. DRYPOINT, 6¾ x 3¾. RIJKS-
MUSEUM, AMSTERDAM.

MASTER OF THE AMSTERDAM CABINET, *The Youth and the Death*. DRYPOINT, S. S.
RIJKSMUSEUM, AMSTERDAM.

Master F. V. B.

END OF THE FIFTEENTH CENTURY, FLEMISH

Master F. V. B. was probably the outstanding Flemish printmaker of his time. Although his manner of engraving seems to show influences of Dürer and Lucas van Leyden, it is not certain that he knew them. His imagery is in the tradition of van der Weyden and Memling. He left fifty-nine plates of great beauty, dealing with a wide selection of subjects, religious and profane.

Master L. C. Z.

END OF FIFTEENTH, BEGINNING OF SIXTEENTH CENTURY

We don't know much of this artist's origin. He was considered first as one of the Netherland masters but lately, on the basis of watermarks and the heraldry, most historians think that he worked in upper Germany, and was born in Bohemia.

MASTER F. V. B., *Judgment of Solomon*. ENGRAVING, 8¾ x 7¼. ROSENWALD COLLECTION, NA-
TIONAL GALLERY OF ART, WASHINGTON, D.C.

MASTER L. C. Z., *The Temptation of Christ*. ENGRAVING, 9 x 6⁹⁄₁₆. ROSENWALD COLLECTION,
NATIONAL GALLERY OF ART, WASHINGTON, D.C.

Master I. A. M.

c. 1440–c. 1504, HOLLAND

Some art historians speculate that Master I. A. M. was Jean de Cologne, painter-engraver who lived in Zwolle. He was also linked to the goldsmith craft and some think that he was a sculptor. He left twenty-six engravings and in some respects he was a forerunner of Lucas van Leyden. Although he is not considered a major master, some of his plates, like "The Mount of Calvary" and "Saint George," are strong and moving statements. I am particularly fond of his pure but expressive draftsmanship.

MASTER I. A. M. OF ZWELLE, *Calvary*. ENGRAVING, 6⅝ x 9. ROSENWALD COLLECTION, NATIONAL GALLERY OF ART, WASHINGTON, D.C.

Martin Schongauer

c. 1430–1491, German

Schongauer was probably born at Colmar and died at Brisach. He was the outstanding figure of German graphic art in the pre-Dürer era, and exerted great influence on the young Dürer who, according to some historians, traveled to Schongauer's studio to enlist as his student, only to find that the master had died.

Schongauer engraved approximately 115 plates, mostly of religious subject matter. Although his style was still Gothic in character, he composed with much greater freedom and in that sense he represents a transition into the Renaissance. The greatness of Schongauer is in the intensity and the evocative power of his imagery.

MARTIN SCHONGAUER, *Christ on the Cross*. ENGRAVING, 4¼ x 2¾. POTTER PALMER COLLECTION, ART INSTITUTE OF CHICAGO.

MARTIN SCHONGAUER, *Flight to Egypt*. ENGRAVING, 10 1/16 x 6 1/2. GIFT OF A. E. FOSTER, YALE UNIVERSITY ART GALLERY, NEW HAVEN.

MARTIN SCHONGAUER, *St. Anthony Tormented by Demons*. ENGRAVING, 12¼ x 8⅜. METRO-
POLITAN MUSEUM OF ART, NEW YORK.

MARTIN SCHONGAUER, *The Censer*. ENGRAVING, 10⅜ x 8⅜. GIFT OF MISS ELIZABETH ACHE-
LIS, YALE UNIVERSITY ART GALLERY, NEW HAVEN.

MARTIN SCHONGAUER, *Death of the Virgin*. ENGRAVING, 10¼ x 6¾. ROSENWALD COLLECTION, NATIONAL GALLERY OF ART, WASHINGTON, D.C.

MARTIN SCHONGAUER, *Crucifixion*. ENGRAVING, 7⅝ x 6. ROSENWALD COLLECTION, NA-
TIONAL GALLERY OF ART, WASHINGTON, D.C.

Israhel van Meckenem

END OF THE FIFTEENTH CENTURY, GERMAN

Van Meckenem was probably the most prolific engraver of the fifteenth century. Approximately 570 engravings are attributed to him. He is a very confusing personality because his large output was a strange mixture of copies, a great deal of commercial work, and, occasionally, prints of great beauty. He copied Schongauer, Dürer, Holbein, and many others. He also bought some of Master E. S.'s plates, reworked them and sold them under his own name for a good profit.

ISRAHEL VAN MECKENEM, *The Five Foxes.* ENGRAVING, 6⅝ x 4⅝. ART INSTITUTE OF CHICAGO.

ISRAHEL VAN MECKENEN, *St. Lucas Painting the Portrait of the Virgin*. ENGRAVING, 8³⁄₁₆ X 5³⁄₄. YALE UNIVERSITY ART GALLERY, NEW HAVEN.

Albrecht Dürer

1471–1528, GERMAN

Dürer's father immigrated from Hungary to Nuremberg. The family
name was changed from the Hungarian Eytas (door) into Thurer
(door in German). His father used the signature Türer, which
eventually was changed into Dürer. Both Dürer's father and uncle
were silversmiths, and as a child he absorbed a love and respect for
ornamental metal work. Dürer was a fine painter but unquestionably
he was one of the greatest and most influential printmakers. In
many respects he was the German counterpart of Leonardo da

ALBRECHT DÜRER, *Descent from the Cross*. ENGRAVING, 4⁹⁄₁₆ X 2¹³⁄₁₆. FRITZ ACHELIS MEM-
ORIAL COLLECTION, YALE UNIVERSITY ART GALLERY, NEW HAVEN.

ALBRECHT DÜRER, *Flight to Egypt*. WOODCUT, 12 x 8⅝. GIFT OF PAUL MELLEN, YALE UNIVERSITY ART GALLERY, NEW HAVEN.

Vinci—a complex, truly Renaissance man, interested in philosophy, science, and art. He was one of the first to break the provincial isolation of Germany. Dürer was interested in Italian art and he was one of the very few German artists admired by the Italians. He exchanged drawings with Raphael and made two trips to Italy. The first trip he made in order to contact fellow artists, the second one to stop the forging of his plates by Marcantonio Raimondi.

Dürer was a great draftsman and an unparalleled virtuoso of metal engraving. He is an interesting example of how the influence of a great artist can be destructive at times. A few artists, like Aldegrever, Baldung, and Barbari, profited by his influence, but lesser talents were corrupted by it. In Dürer's hand technical virtuosity always served expression; with most of his followers it became

ALBRECHT DÜRER, *Dancing Peasants.* ENGRAVING, 4⅝ x 2¹⁵⁄₁₆. FRITZ ACHELIS MEMORIAL COLLECTION, YALE UNIVERSITY ART COLLECTION, NEW HAVEN.

an end in itself. This of course doesn't alter his stature as one of the greatest artists of his time. We can't judge Dürer for the sins of his followers, as we can't hold Rembrandt responsible for all the horrible pictures painted under his influence.

Dürer was a great image maker. His imagination poured out torrents of the most unbelievable pictorial inventions. His lines, pitching, darting, and cascading performed a magic dance of the graphic arts. He was at his best in his sensitive and personal metal engravings. Although these prints are incredibly rich in details, a shimmering silken light gives them unity. Dürer also made a few etchings. They are rich and powerful images but lack the sensitive control of his engravings. This is due to the fact that in Dürer's time etching in stages had not yet developed. As the whole plate

ALBRECHT DÜRER, FROM THE "SMALL PASSION." ENGRAVING ON COPPER, 3 X 4¾. FRITZ ACHELIS MEMORIAL COLLECTION, YALE UNIVERSITY ART GALLERY, NEW HAVEN.

was etched only once, he couldn't control the subtle linear modulations. He also made two drypoints of great beauty. Beside his extensive metal work, Dürer also published over three hundred woodcuts. In this art form his most important publications were: "The Apocalypse," "The Great Passion," "The Small Passion," and "The Life of the Virgin." Among his many decorative designs the triumphal arch of the Emperor Maximilian is the most impressive. As far as we know most of these blocks were cut by craftsmen after the designs of Dürer. In spite of this, his imagery has such visionary power and his drawing is so expressive that even the reproductive cutting could not destroy their magic.

ALBRECHT DÜRER, *The Cannon*. ETCHING, $8^{17}\!/_{32}$ X $12^{19}\!/_{32}$. LIBRARY OF CONGRESS, WASHINGTON, D.C.

ALBRECHT DÜRER, *Knight, Death and Devil*. ENGRAVING, 9¾ x 7⅜. BROOKLYN MUSEUM.

ALBRECHT DÜRER, *St. Jerome and the Willow Tree*. DRYPOINT, 8⅜ x 7⅜. METROPOLITAN MUSEUM OF ART, NEW YORK.

ALBRECHT DÜRER, *St. Eustice*. ENGRAVING, 14⅛ x 10¼. BROOKLYN MUSEUM.

ALBRECHT DÜRER, FROM THE "APOCALYPSE." WOODCUT, 15⅞ x 11⅜. GIFT OF PAUL MELLON, YALE UNIVERSITY ART GALLERY, NEW HAVEN.

ALBRECHT DÜRER, *The Rape of a Young Woman*. ENGRAVING, 12¼ x 8⅜. FLETCHER FUND, METROPOLITAN MUSEUM OF ART, NEW YORK.

Albrecht Altdorfer

c. 1480–1538, GERMAN

Painter, engraver, and architectural designer, Altdorfer was born near Altdorf and worked in Ratisbonne where he died. In his lifetime he produced nearly one hundred line engravings on copper and approximately fifty woodcuts. He is one of the most original artists of his period. I find particularly exciting his treatment of landscapes. Altdorfer deserves much greater recognition than he ever got.

ALBRECHT ALTDORFER, *Virgin and Child*. ENGRAVING, 6⁷⁄₁₆ x 4⁹⁄₁₆. ROGERS FUND, METROPOLITAN MUSEUM OF ART, NEW YORK.

ALBRECHT ALTDORFER, *Pine*. ETCHING, 6⅝ x 4⅞. LIBRARY OF CONGRESS, WASHINGTON, D.C.

ALBRECHT ALTDORFER, *The Annunciation*. WOODCUT, 4¾ x 3²³⁄₃₂. HARRIS BRISBANE DICK
FUND, METROPOLITAN MUSEUM OF ART, NEW YORK.

ALBRECHT ALTDORFER, *Holy Family at a Fountain*. WOODCUT, 9 x 6$\frac{29}{32}$. ROGERS FUND,
METROPOLITAN MUSEUM OF ART, NEW YORK.

Heinrich Aldegrever

1502–c. 1558, GERMAN

Painter, engraver, and student of Dürer, Aldegrever was born at Paderborn but worked in Nuremberg for many years of his life. He is a minor master of his period and produced nearly three hundred plates. Although his engravings were strongly influenced by Dürer and Marcantonio Raimondi, he achieved a personal expression. His drawing was elegant but strong. His sensitive treatment of light and dark allowed him to introduce unbelievably intricate ornamental passages into his prints without destroying their unity.

HEINRICH ALDEGREVER, *Lot Protecting the Angels*. ENGRAVING, 4½ x 3¼. BROOKLYN MUSEUM.

Lucas Cranach the Elder

1472–1553, GERMAN

Cranach is one of the most representative figures of the German
Renaissance. He was earthy and fun loving, not an intellectual like
Dürer. This made him much less vulnerable to the Italian influence.
He had a big workshop in Wittenberg where, during a long life, he
produced an enormous amount of paintings, many woodcuts, and a
few metal engravings.

LUCAS CRANACH, *Crowning of Christ.* WOODCUT, 9¾ x 6⅝. YALE UNIVERSITY ART GALLERY,
NEW HAVEN.

LUCAS CRANACH, *Temptation of St. Anthony*. WOODCUT, 16⅛ x 10⅝. GIFT OF J. S. MORGAN, METROPOLITAN MUSEUM OF ART, NEW YORK.

Hans Grien Baldung

c. 1476–1545, GERMAN

Baldung was a painter, engraver of Schwab origin. He was born near Strasbourg where he worked with a student of Schoengauer. Later he moved to Nuremberg where he studied with Dürer from 1511 to 1518. He was one of the most original artists of his time. In his hallucinatory images of witchcraft and magic he expressed the lingering medievial mysticism present in the German Renaissance. Confronted with Baldung's powerful imagery it is difficult to understand why he wasn't held in higher esteem by art history. Probably the main reason was the domination of European aesthetics by the Italian Renaissance. German art was coarse, brutal, angular, and ugly to a taste accustomed to the sweet, idealized, mellow images of Italian art. The popularity of Dürer outside of Germany was an exception because to some degree his work represented a compromise between the German and the Italian expression.

HANS GRIEN BALDUNG, *The Witches Sabbath*. CHIAROSCURO WOODCUT, $14\frac{11}{16}$ x $10\frac{1}{8}$. GIFT OF FELIX M. WARBURG, METROPOLITAN MUSEUM OF ART, NEW YORK.

HANS GRIEN BALDUNG, *Seven Horses Fighting*. WOODCUT, 8½ x 12¾. HARRIS BRISBANE
DICK FUND, METROPOLITAN MUSEUM OF ART, NEW YORK.

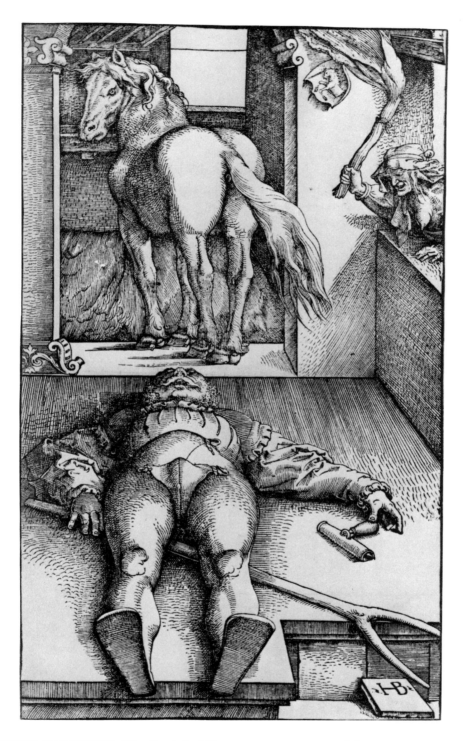

HANS GRIEN BALDUNG, *The Bewitched Groom*. WOODCUT, 13 X 7¼. YALE UNIVERSITY ART
GALLERY, NEW HAVEN.

Pieter Brueghel the Elder

c. 1520–1569, Flemish

Pieter the Elder was a great painter, and one of the greatest draftsman who ever lived. He was a complex figure whose life's work combined the fantastic world of Bosch with earthy interpretations of Flemish peasant life. His engravings are skillful reproductions of his designs but without the sensibility and spark always present in his drawings. There is only one etching, "The Wild Rabbit Hunt," that can be directly attributed to him. If we compare this print with the engravings published under his name, it becomes unmistakenly clear that even the most skillful craftsman can't preserve in a copy the sensitivity of an original drawing.

PIETER (THE ELDER) BRUEGHEL, *Rabbit Hunt*. ETCHING, 8¾ x 11½. RIJKSMUSEUM, AMSTERDAM.

Lucas van Leyden

1494–1533, DUTCH

Lucas van Leyden was the Mozart of engraving. He started to engrave at the age of nine, and at the age of fourteen he engraved "Mahomet and the Monk," a plate that not only shows his superb draftsmanship and engraving technique, but also his creative powers. Although he was influenced by Dürer in the beginning, he soon developed a personal style, delicate and fluid. The most characteristic qualities of the Leyden prints are a presence of light and great elegance. The contemporary copies of his work lack these qualities and by comparison they are mechanical.

LUCAS VAN LEYDEN, *David Playing the Harp before Saul*. ENGRAVING, 10 X 7¼. ROGERS FUND, METROPOLITAN MUSEUM OF ART, NEW YORK.

LUCAS VAN LEYDEN, *The Prodidgal Son*. ENGRAVING, 7⅛ x 9¾. BROOKLYN MUSEUM.

LUCAS VAN LEYDEN, *The Milkmaid*. ENGRAVING, 4½ x 6⅛. HARRIS BRISBANE DICK FUND,
METROPOLITAN MUSEUM OF ART, NEW YORK.

Hans Holbein the Younger

c. 1497–1543, German

A great painter and draftsman, he produced a vast number of woodcuts. Holbein made the designs but to our knowledge he never cut
the blocks himself. In spite of this, his superb draftsmanship and
pictorial inventiveness are evident. I am particularly fond of his
"Dance of Death" series.

HANS (THE YOUNGER) HOLBEIN, THREE WOODCUTS FROM THE "DANCE OF DEATH": *The
Soldier*, 2⁹⁄₁₆ x 2; *The Bride*, 2½ x 2; *The Countess*, 2⁹⁄₁₆ x 2. ROGERS FUND, METROPOLITAN
MUSEUM OF ART, NEW YORK.

Jean Duvet

1485–1561, FRENCH

Duvet was born in Langres and worked most of his life in Dijon. He was a goldsmith. Influenced by Dürer, he produced two major sets of prints: "La Licorne" (c.1560) and "L'Apocalypse" (c.1561). Duvet is one of the most interesting and enigmatic figures of the history of printmaking. Like Grunewald, he is a rediscovery of the twentieth century. We know little about him and he didn't leave an extensive *oeuvre*. Duvet's manner of engraving and his concept of shallow space was obviously conditioned by his training as a goldsmith. He loved ornamentation and often overcharged his compositions with them, but his visionary powers and personal imagery makes him one of the great printmakers.

JEAN DUVET, *The Crucifixion*. ENGRAVING, 12¼ x 8⅝. CLARENCE BUCKINGHAM COLLECTION,
ART INSTITUTE OF CHICAGO.

JEAN DUVET, *The Angel Sounding the Sixth Trumpet* (FROM "THE APOCALYPSE"). ENGRAVING, $11\frac{3}{4}$ x $8\frac{1}{2}$. YALE UNIVERSITY ART GALLERY, NEW HAVEN.

JEAN DUVET, *Marriage of Adam and Eve.* ENGRAVING, 11 13/16 x 8⅜. HARRIS BRISBANE DICK FUND, METROPOLITAN MUSEUM OF ART, NEW YORK.

Rembrandt van Rijn

1606–1669, DUTCH

Among the greatest artists of the West Rembrandt occupies a very special place. His name became synonymous with genius, and no great artist, with the exception of Picasso, inspired the making of so many bad pictures and prints as Rembrandt. His world is so unique, his style so personal, that followers could only imitate his mannerism without the substance of his work. The dramatic interplay of light and dark so identified with Rembrandt became over-dramatized theater in the hand of his imitators. He did not illustrate light, his paintings and prints radiated an inner glow.

The fast whiplash of his pen stroke flooded with rich washes seduced many young artists who did not realize that unbelievable precision lay hidden under his spontaneous manner.

The Rembrandt print was abused in the same manner. Any printmaker who made a dark print felt that he was following the master's footsteps. The black print with dramatic highlights became the trademark of genius.

REMBRANDT VAN RIJN, *Self-portrait of Youth*. ETCHING, 3 X 3. RIJKSMUSEUM, AMSTERDAM.

REMBRANDT VAN RIJN, *St. Jerome*. ETCHING, 7¼ x 5¼. BROOKLYN MUSEUM.

Nothing makes one more aware of verbal limitations than trying to analyze the greatness of Rembrandt. To list the ingredients of his talent is meaningless. Many other artists had them and they didn't add up to Rembrandt. To say that his method of over-lapping shallow, successive bites created luminous darks, has nothing to do with the substance of his imagery. Probably the only way it is possible to verbalize the intangibles of the visual arts is by creating a poetic equivalent. Unfortunately there are few Baudelaires.

Rembrandt the printmaker wasn't an extraordinary technician. Any commercial engraver of his time was better than he, and compared to our knowledge of craft today, he was a primitive. Yet I wonder how many prints of our time will be remembered one hundred years from now.

Remembrandt made approximately three hundred etchings. Some of his plates may have been lost, some were worked over after his death by his students, worked over beyond recognition. In his later periods he used drypoint exclusively to sketch in details and

REMBRANDT VAN RIJN, *Rembrandt's Mother*. ETCHING, 2¹¹⁄₁₆ X 2⁹⁄₃₂. ROGERS FUND, METROPOLITAN MUSEUM OF ART, NEW YORK.

to reinforce dark accents. He often reworked his plates between printings, thus his proofs show great variation. Many Rembrandt prints are as unique as a monoprint.

One of the greatest charms of Rembrandt is his unaffected intimacy. Some geniuses are remote and forbidding. Rembrandt invites us into his life to share his joys, his ecstasies, and his sorrows. He doesn't show himself in his Sunday best only, but lets us see him in naked reality.

I had a great problem in selecting the Rembrandt prints for this book. I prefer to show lesser known prints, yet to leave out some of his important work is impossible without fatally weakening his impact. I included, however, a few of his lesser known earthy prints in order to show the depth and variety of his *oeuvre*.

REMBRANDT VAN RIJN, *Man Passing Water*. ETCHING, 2 X 3½. RIJKSMUSEUM, AMSTERDAM.

REMBRANDT VAN RIJN, *Christ Presented to the People*. ETCHING, 14$\frac{1}{16}$ X 18. FRITZ ACHELIS
MEMORIAL COLLECTION, YALE UNIVERSITY ART COLLECTION, NEW HAVEN.

REMBRANDT VAN RIJN, *Christ Presented to the People*. ETCHING, DRYPOINT. DETAIL, LOWER LEFT CORNER OF EARLY STATE. GIFT OF FELIX M. WARBURG, METROPOLITAN MUSEUM OF ART, NEW YORK.

REMBRANDT VAN RIJN, *The Three Crosses*. ETCHING, DRYPOINT, 3RD STATE. 15¼ x 18¼.
CLARENCE BUCKINGHAM COLLECTION, ART INSTITUTE OF CHICAGO.

REMBRANDT VAN RIJN, *The Three Crosses*. ETCHING, DRYPOINT, 4TH STATE. DETAIL. METRO-
POLITAN MUSEUM OF ART, NEW YORK.

REMBRANDT VAN RIJN, *Close-up of Trees with a Vista*. DRYPOINT, 4⅞ x 8⅛. BROOKLYN MUSEUM.

REMBRANDT VAN RIJN, *Christ Preaching*. ETCHING, 6¼ x 8¼. GIFT OF HAROLD K. HOCHS-
CHILD, BROOKLYN MUSEUM.

REMBRANDT VAN RIJN, *Rembrandt's Mother*. ETCHING, 5⅝ X 5. BROOKLYN MUSEUM.

REMBRANDT VAN RIJN, *Self-portrait with Fur Cap*. ETCHING, 2¾ X 2¾. RIJKSMUSEUM, AMSTERDAM.

REMBRANDT VAN RIJN, *Self-portrait Whistling*. ETCHING, 2¹³⁄₁₆ X 2¼. RIJKSMUSEUM, AMSTERDAM.

Hercules Seghers

c. 1589–c. 1638, Dutch

Seghers is one of the strangest and most tragic figures in the history of art. He was a visionary and a great innovator who left behind him a number of plates so unusual in style and in technique that they still baffle most experts. He was a contemporary and friend of Rembrandt; one of the few who appreciated him and bought some

HERCULES SEGHERS, *Landscape with Two Steeples*. ETCHING, 5⅜ x 4. RIJKSMUSEUM, AMSTERDAM.

of his prints. Rembrandt even reworked one of Seghers' plates, "Tobias and the Angel." Scraping the figures out and replacing them with others it became "The Flight into Egypt." Some feel that this was a questionable improvement.

Seghers was the first real experimenter in intaglio color printing. He printed on tinted canvas with colors, tried light lines on dark backgrounds and at times mixed printing with hand coloring. It is hard to tell what motivated his research in this direction, it was so totally out of tune with his time and environment. Some claim that, driven by desperation and misery, he became obsessed with the idea that an invention of "printed painting" would solve his financial problems. Maybe so, although I am always leery when the experts offer their pragmatic explanations to "eccentricity" they can't understand, as when they say that Greco elongated his figures because he was astigmatic.

HERCULES SEGHERS, *Rocky Landscape with a Plateau*. ETCHING, 4⅜ x 5⅝. METROPOLITAN MUSEUM OF ART, NEW YORK.

Most of Seghers' etchings represented craggy, acrid landscapes, desolate as the moon. Everything he has drawn, landscapes, still lifes, even figures, seem to be made of stone. It is a world suspended in the timelessness of death. No wonder poor Seghers couldn't sell them.

The etching technique of Seghers was very unorthodox in itself. His eroded lines, so well suited to his subject matter, are unlike any etched line made before him. As a matter of fact, only contemporary etching technique produces anything comparable. This led some experts to the conclusion that Seghers must have invented the lift ground, an aquatint technique. So far, nothing conclusive has come out of these investigations. Frankly, I don't much care; I am grateful for the legacy of these strangely moving images.

The only comprehensive collection of Seghers prints is in the Rijksmuseum in Amsterdam.

HERCULES SEGHERS, *The Rocky River Landscape*. ETCHING, 6⅞ x 8½. RIJKSMUSEUM, AMSTERDAM.

Jacob van Ruisdael

c. 1628–1682, Dutch

Ruisdael was born and died near Haarlem. He was a great landscape painter, and was one of those who succeeded in making it a major art form. This again brings up the nonsense of classifying art forms into major and minor categories. I discussed this in my introduction in relation to various media, but it is equally untenable in relation to subject matter. A small landscape of Cézanne has more significance than all the great historic paintings of the nineteenth century.

Ruisdael made only thirteen etchings. However, some of them rank with the best of his time. These sensitively drawn landscapes are fresh and convincing. They are not the stereotype theatrical background landscapes. In their atmospheric quality they herald the Fontainebleau school.

JACOB VAN RUISDAEL, *House with Trees Alongside a River*. ETCHING, APPROX. 7 X 11. RIJKSMUSEUM, AMSTERDAM.

JACOB VAN RUISDAEL, *The Traveller*. ETCHING, 7¼ x 10¹¹⁄₁₆. HARRIS BRISBANE DICK FUND,
METROPOLITAN MUSEUM OF ART, NEW YORK.

Anthony Van Dyck

1599–1641, DUTCH

Van Dyck was Rubens' outstanding student. He was a great painter
and a superb draftsman. At the age of twenty-seven he undertook a
very ambitious project: the etched portraits of the one hundred most
famous men of his day. This set of prints is known as the "Iconog-
raphy." He completed eighteen portraits but only five of these remained unchanged ("Peter Breughel the Younger," "Snellinx,"
"Erasmus," "Suttermans," and "Josse de Momper"); another five
were retouched by professional engravers, and the rest were completely reworked by them. In comparing the prints made by Van
Dyck with the other plates, one realizes the deadliness of this type
of professionalism—of craftsmanship without sensibility. The reworked plates are without the creative vitality of Van Dyck's own
drawings. I reproduce "Erasmus," a plate covered with etching
mistakes, yet a completely convincing, sensitive work of art.

ANTHONY VAN DYCK, *Portrait of Erasmus*. DETAIL. COLLECTION OF MR. AND MRS. BERNARD
CHAET.

Eraſmus Rotterdamus.

Ant. van Dyck fecit aqua forti.

ANTHONY VAN DYCK, *Portrait of Erasmus*. ETCHING, 9½ x 6. COLLECTION OF MR. AND MRS. BERNARD CHAET.

A la fin ces Voleurs infames et perdus ,
Comme fruits malheureux a cet arbre pendus

Monstrent bien que le crime (horrible et noire engeance)
Est luy mesme instrument de honte et de vengeance ,

Et que c'est le Destin des hommes vicieux
Desprouuer tost ou tard la iustice des Cieux . 11

Jacques Callot

1592–1635, French

Callot was a great illustrator of his time. Like Hogarth later on in England, Callot not only recorded the customs, historical events, and morals of his time but forcefully commented on them. He revolutionized the art of etching and his innovations influenced generations of printmakers, including Rembrandt. He originated the use of the echope, a tool with which he could approximate the elegant swelling and tapering character of the engraved line in etching. This practice was always severely criticized by purists and to my knowledge not used by any fine artist today. Most of Callot's prints are rather manneristic and decorative. I consider "The Temptation of St. Anthony" and part of "The Miseries and Disasters of War" his best work. In these prints he transcends mere illustrations into powerful images of universal significance.

JACQUES CALLOT, *Le Pendaison* (FROM "LES GRANDES MISERES DE LA GUERRE"). ETCHING, $3\frac{7}{32}$ X $7\frac{5}{16}$. ROGERS FUND, METROPOLITAN MUSEUM OF ART, NEW YORK.

JACQUES CALLOT, *The Temptation of St. Anthony*. ETCHING, $12\frac{3}{8}$ x $18\frac{1}{4}$. YALE UNIVERSITY
ART GALLERY, NEW HAVEN.

Antonio (Canaletto) Canal

1697–1768, ITALIAN

Canaletto was a great Venetian landscape painter. His lyrical etchings are flooded with the same light that we identify with his paintings. They are marvelous examples of how a great draftsman can create color and light with graphic means. The Canaletto etchings are practically inexhaustible in linear and textural inventions.

ANTONIO CANAL (CANALETTO), *La Terre di Malghera*. ETCHING. DETAIL. GIFT OF EDWARD B. GREENE, YALE UNIVERSITY ART GALLERY, NEW HAVEN.

ANTONIO CANAL (CANALETTO), *La Terre di Malghera*. ETCHING, 11¾ x 16⅞. GIFT
OF EDWARD B. GREENE, YALE UNIVERSITY ART GALLERY, NEW HAVEN.

Giovanni Battista Tiepolo

1696–1770, ITALIAN

Tiepolo was one of the great virtuosos of eighteenth-century Italian painting. He was primarily a muralist, and with the aid of his two sons Domenico and Lorenzo, was one of the most prolific and successful painters of his time. Because of his countless decorative panels Tiepolo was not thought of as a serious artist for a long time. Lately, together with the mannerists, there is a re-evaluation of Tiepolo as an artist. Unquestionably, he was a superb draftsman and his sketches for his murals are treasured by collectors of fine drawings. He made some etchings, thirty-eight plates altogether. I am particularly interested in his sensitivity to light, in his capacity to create a breathing luminous space in his prints. Tiepolo was an important influence on Goya.

GIOVANNI BATTISTA TIEPOLO, *Adoration of the Kings*. ETCHING, 17¼ X 11⅜. RIJKSMUSE-
UM, AMSTERDAM.

Giambattista Piranesi

1720–1778, ITALIAN

Piranesi, the great Venetian printmaker, is a rather interesting figure in the history of printmaking. He was educated as an architect and was passionately interested in Roman antiquities. He spent most of his time in Rome doing archaeological research and completed the incredible number of three thousand large etchings. Although these plates on architecture and antiquities are extremely competent and some of them even lift themselves into poetic imagery, his lasting fame rests upon a series of sixteen large etchings, the "Carceri D' Invenzione" (imaginery prison scenes) made in his youth. These prints are so personal, so rich in color and light, so evocative in mood that they far surpass in interest anything that he created after them. Unfortunately he was too far ahead of his time: the popular taste of his era could not appreciate the significance of these images. Discouraged, Piranesi never again attempted anything of comparable significance.

VEDUTA *del Sotterranee Fondamento del Maufoleo, che fu eretto da Elio* .... *Adriano Imp.* ... *In queſta parte, la quali è eſpoſta alla Facciata, gli Speroni ſono tutti coſtruiti di groſſi Travertini* . *A Parte di Riempitura, ovvero ſia di* .... *Opera incerta a corſi la quale veſte d'oſmi intorno il Fondati.* B *Palizzate.* C *Parte del Mauſoleo.*

GIAMBATTISTA PIRANESI, *Foundation of Hadrian's Tomb*. ENGRAVING, 28 X 19. ROGERS
FUND, METROPOLITAN MUSEUM OF ART, NEW YORK.

GIAMBATTISTA PIRANESI, FROM THE "CARCERIO." ETCHING, 16¼ x 21½. HARRIS BRISBANE
DICK FUND, METROPOLITAN MUSEUM OF ART, NEW YORK.

GIAMBATTISTA PIRANESI, FROM THE "CARCERIO." ETCHING, 21⅜ x 16¼. HARRIS BRISBANE
DICK FUND, METROPOLITAN MUSEUM OF ART, NEW YORK.

William Hogarth

1697–1764, ENGLISH

Hogarth was an English pictorial satirist. In many respects his work belongs to the tradition of Callot and Daumier, but he is much more earthy and vulgar than Callot and lacks the bitterness of Daumier. Hogarth was really a printmaker of the people; his work was so popular that he had to protect it with a copyright act. He instigated this first protective measure of artists' rights, which was passed by the English Parliament in 1735. Hogarth's most important publications were "The Harlot's Progress" and "The Rake's Progress." I personally like best his plates illustrating the street life in London. These prints reveal sharp observation projected with great visual power and vitality.

WILLIAM HOGARTH, *The Cockpit*. ENGRAVING, 12½ x 15¼. DETAIL. BROOKLYN MUSEUM.

WILLIAM HOGARTH, *Southwark Fair*. ENGRAVING, $14\frac{1}{4}$ x $18\frac{1}{2}$. BROOKLYN MUSEUM.

Francisco Jose de Goya y Lucientes

1746–1828, SPANISH

Goya is one of the towering figures of European art. Really to know him one must visit the Prado Museum in Madrid. There, walking through seven rooms filled with his paintings, his drawings, his prints, one lives through two centuries. The young Goya is a typical eighteenth-century painter influenced by Italian art. His early work is joyful and decorative and not very personal. As he matures he responds more and more to his Spanish environment, full of intrigue and violence. Beginning with elegant courtiers and happy dancing peasants we come to a world haunted by the bloody ghosts of wars and inquisitions. Finally, at the end we find "The Black Goyas," the terrifying visions of a deaf old man. He painted these on the walls of the house in which he lived alone in a self-imposed exile surrounded by monsters of his own imagination.

Goya the printmaker is a particularly interesting phenomenon. Before him Spain had no great tradition in the graphic arts. Goya's interest in prints probably started with his voyage to Italy. Unquestionably he learned a great deal from Tiepolo. He definitely learned the technique of the aquatint from him, but even his etched lines show this influence. Goya created four important cycles of prints. The first, "Los Caprichos," 1793–99, contains eighty enigmatic prints commenting on all phases of life. These prints are a fascinating conglomeration of biting satire, historical allegory, and soaring fantasy. Above all, they are evocative images of supreme craftsmanship and plasticity.

In 1810, inspired by the war of independence, he started working on "Los Desastres de la Guerra." He made eighty-three plates of burning protest and condemnation of the brutality and the stupidity of war. The intensity of these prints result in an impression of almost unbearable violence. In comparison, Jacques Callot's famous prints on the same subject, "The Miseries and Disasters of War," seem like polite ballroom scenes.

FRANCISCO GOYA, *Self-portrait* (FROM "LOS CAPRICHOS"). ETCHING, 5¼ x 4⅜. BROOKLYN MUSEUM.

After "The Disasters of the War," Goya made thirty-three plates depicting the art of bullfighting, "La Tauromaquia." In these he expressed with clarity and force the ritualistic attitude of the Spanish people toward the bullfight. These are not illustrations of a national sport but haunting images of a bloody religious ceremony.

The "Proverbs" or "Disparates" was Goya's last important cycle of prints. These images are even more mysterious and disturbing than the "Caprichos." They are satires on human folly and misery, projected on a scale that is superhuman. Counting the odd prints and a few lithographs, Goya produced in his lifetime approximately 260 prints.

Technically the Goya prints are simple and direct. In most of his plates he combined hard-ground etching with aquatint. Although in his time aquatint was a new medium, he used it with great understanding. The rich color orchestration of his prints is achieved by the interplay of line etching with aquatinted tonal passages. His greatness, however, has little to do with his technical skill. He was an *innovator*, and he could communicate with incredible impact. Goya is still one of the most powerful influences in figurative art.

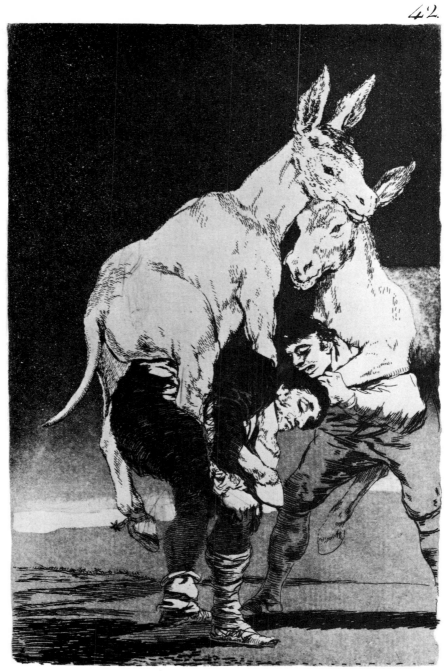

Tu que no puedes.

FRANCISCO GOYA, *Tu Que No Puedes* (FROM "LOS CAPRICHOS"). ETCHING, 8½ x 6. BROOKLYN MUSEUM.

Ensayos.

FRANCISCO GOYA, *Ensayos* (FROM "LOS CAPRICHOS"). ETCHING, 8¼ x 6½. BROOKLYN MU
SEUM.

Donde vá mama

FRANCISCO GOYA, *Donde vá Mama* (FROM "LOS CAPRICHOS"). ETCHING, 8½ x 6⅝. BROOKLYN MUSEUM.

Siempre sucede.

FRANCISCO GOYA, *Siempre Sucede* (FROM "LOS DESASTRES DE LA GUERRA"). ETCHING, 9⅜ X 13.
YALE UNIVERSITY ART GALLERY, NEW HAVEN.

Se aprovechan.

FRANCISCO GOYA, *Se Aprovechan* (FROM "LOS DESASTRES DE LA GUERRA"). ETCHING, 9⅜ X 13.
YALE UNIVERSITY ART GALLERY, NEW HAVEN.

Dibersion de España.

FRANCISCO GOYA, *Dibersion de España*. LITHOGRAPH, 12 X 16⅜. ROGERS FUND. METROPOLITAN
MUSEUM OF ART, NEW YORK.

FRANCISCO GOYA, *Bravo Toro*. LITHOGRAPH, $12\frac{1}{4}$ x $16\frac{3}{8}$. ROGERS FUND, METROPOLITAN
MUSEUM OF AFT, NEW YORK.

William Blake

1757–1827, ENGLISH

Poet and printmaker, Blake was a real visionary, deeply influenced
by the Gothic and the Middle Ages. He belongs to that rare species
of solitary figures whose development is unrelated to the mainstream
of art history. Practically all his prints were book illustrations. He
often used a relief etching method invented by himself to print the
text and the image on the same plate. William Hayter, the great
contemporary English printmaker, did a great deal of research into
the Blake technique and revived it at his school, Atelier 17.

WILLIAM BLAKE, *The Whirlwind of Lovers* (ILLUSTRATION TO DANTE'S *Inferno*). ENGRAVING,
9⅜ x 13³⁄₁₆. ROGERS FUND, METROPOLITAN MUSEUM OF ART, NEW YORK.

Hanabusa Itcho

1652–1724, JAPANESE

Itcho is not too well known, yet he was one of the great satirical artists of Japanese art. He was banished for twelve years as punishment for one of his satirical prints. He kept working on his island prison and many of his prints were published in books after his death. The freshness of his drawings, his graphic inventiveness, and his humor makes Itcho's work a pure delight.

HANABUSA ITCHO, *Pages from a book.* WOODCUT, 8 x 13. AUTHOR'S COLLECTION.

Okumura Masanobu

1689–1756, JAPANESE

One of the most important innovators in Japanese printmaking, Masanobu invented the two-color print and generally standardized color printing. His studio became the greatest influence on the evolution of the Japanese woodcut.

The following innovations are identified with him: the urushi; rendering the black printing ink lacquer-like by using a glue (uikava); the "blind pressing" of deepened lines into limed surfaces. This technique approximated the "Tosa" lacquer printings.

Masanobu was the first to combine gold and silver overlay on his blacks. He was also one of the first to use the red "beni" on his prints.

Masanobu was the first to standardize the popular red-green hand-colored prints by developing separate blocks for each color.

The "uki" (near and far) picture was Masanobu's experiment with perspective. He was also the first to make triptychs and the elongated "hashira-ye" or doorpost pictures.

OKUMURA MASANOBU, COLOR WOODCUT. FLETCHER FUND, METROPOLITAN MUSEUM OF ART,
NEW YORK.

Toshusai Sharaku

DATE OF BIRTH AND DEATH UNKNOWN

WORKED 1793–? , JAPANESE

Sharaku is not only one of the greatest but also the most mysterious figures of Japanese art. He came from nowhere. Suddenly, his magnificent, powerful portraits of actors appeared as posters. These portraits were revolutionary in many ways. Their boldness, verging on caricature, their psychological insight, their richness of color, all represented a daring new attitude. The originality of these prints disturbed the authorities to the point that the police prohibited them. In less than two years of his working life, Sharaku produced approximately three hundred portraits of actors in their various roles. Then this prodigious flow of work stopped, and he disappeared. All we know is that his real name probably was Saito Jurobei, a "No" player. But where did he study? Why didn't anyone know him before 1793? Where did he go afterward? One thing is sure: the Japanese did not understand him. He is a European discovery. In 1890 he is listed in a book by Bing as one of the greatest Japanese artists. In a Japanese book, *Masterpieces of the Ukiyo-ye School*, published in 1900, he is not even mentioned. Of all Japanese art, Sharaku's prints are some of the rarest and most sought-after today.

TOSHUSAI SHARAKU, *Segava Kikunojo III as O-Shizu*. WOODCUT, 14⅞ x 9. BROOKLYN MU-
SEUM.

TOSHUSAI SHARAKU, *Azaiki Rijkuso*. COLOR WOODCUT, 14⅝ x 9¾. BROOKLYN MUSEUM.

TOSHUSAI SHARAKU, *Ichikawa Ebizo*. COLOR WOODCUT, 14⅝ x 9½. BROOKLYN MUSEUM.

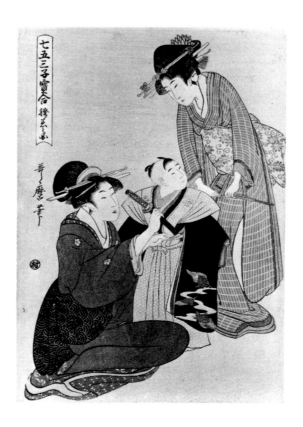

Kitagawa Utamaro

c. 1754–1806, Japanese

I think that Utamaro can justly be called the great poet of Japanese art. Utamaro's prints are the most perfect expressions of a tender, loving contemplation of nature. To the Japanese, nature is beauty whether it is seen in a flowering branch, a dragonfly, or a fragile child-woman of the Yoshiwara. Utamaro's art is an eloquent testimony to this concept. He didn't merely illustrate beauty and nature: he re-created them in his elegant dancing, flowing lines. Toward the end of his life, at the height of his career, age fifty, he was put in jail for an offending print. Broken in body and spirit, he died shortly after his release. This was the brutal end of the most tender artist Japan ever had. During his relatively short life, Utamaro produced over six hundred series of books and albums.

KITAGAWA UTAMARO, *Dressing a Boy*. COLOR WOODCUT, 15½ x 10½. BROOKLYN MUSEUM.

KITAGAWA UTAMARO, PAGE FROM HIS BOOK ON WOMEN MAKING UP. COLOR WOODCUT, 14½ x 9¾. AUTHOR'S COLLECTION.

Katsushika Hokusai

1760–1849, JAPANESE

Hokusai, the most famous master of the woodcut, was born in Honjo, a suburb of Yedo. He lived a long life. From the age of thirteen when he became an apprentice in a wood-carving studio in Yokaomi, until his death, he poured out an unending stream of masterpieces. He produced 35,000 drawings and prints, a staggering figure even if we consider his unusually long life. The fact that besides his paintings he also wrote books and numerous poems seems incredible.

From the beginning of his career, when he called himself Tetsuzo, Hokusai kept adopting fancy names. It was a Japanese tradition that pupils often adopted their master's name or the name of a person they admired. Hokusai, however, outdid all of them. He used approximately fifty names during his lifetime. To keep track of all his activities, his constant moving about (he lived in ninety-two dwellings during his lifetime), requires real detective work.

There are few masters in the history of art whose work is comparable to Hokusai's in variety and depth. Perhaps one could draw a parallel between Goya and Hokusai in the sense that both started out as classicists and finished as innovators.

Hokusai's interests encompassed everything from Japanese history and mythology, to popular customs, sex habits, animal life, and landscape.

He was an indefatigable observer, who would record with expressive powers the living and the dead world.

Because of Hokusai's enormous output and the variety of his work it is impossible to give a complete representation of his art within the limitations of this volume. I did my best to select enough variety to give an inkling of his universality. The thirty-six "Views of Mount Fuji" is probably the most popular set of prints Hokusai ever published. They are the most sought after, the most frequently published, and probably the most expensive of his prints. I show only one of these. I was always much more fascinated by his books, the fifteen volumes of *Mangwa*, filled with informal sketches of anything and everything that came to his mind. These are much more

revealing than his formal paintings, very much like the Leonardo sketches; they tell more about his genius than his finished work. I also love the study books he published to teach drawing—the "Sashin Gwafu" nature drawings, the "Hokusai Sogwa," rough drawings, the "Denshin Gwakio" (Mirror of Drawings), and the "Kwacho Gaden" filled with his animal and plant studies. These books can still be bought for fairly reasonable prices although many of them were destroyed by dealers who cut them up to sell the individual pages for huge profit.

KATSUSHIKA HOKUSAI, *Lightning at the Foot of the Fuji.* COLOR WOODCUT, 9⅞ x 14⅝. BROOKLYN MUSEUM.

KATSUSHIKA HOKUSAI, FROM THE "MANGWA." WOODCUT, 6¾ x 4⅞. GIFT OF HOWARD
MANSFIELD, METROPOLITAN MUSEUM OF ART, NEW YORK.

KATSUSHIKA HOKUSAI, FROM THE "MANGWA." WOODCUT, 6¾ x 4⅞. GIFT OF HOWARD
MANSFIELD, METROPOLITAN MUSEUM OF ART, NEW YORK.

KATSUSHIKA HOKUSAI, *Storm* (FROM "THE 100 VIEWS OF FUJI"). WOODCUT, 7¼ X 5. GIFT OF
HOWARD MANSFIELD, METROPOLITAN MUSEUM OF ART, NEW YORK.

UTAGAWA HIROSHIGE I, *Shower on O-Haski Bridge.* COLOR WOODCUT, 13¼ x 8⅛. BROOK-
LYN MUSEUM.

Utagawa Ando Hiroshige

1797–1858, JAPANESE

Hiroshige was a great landscape painter of Japan and the last truly great printmaker of the remarkable dynasty that started about two centuries before his death. He was one of the first Japanese artists appreciated in Europe, and his influence did a great deal to popularize Eastern art in the West. He was already a famous artist in Europe when in Japan he was known mostly as a poet.

Hiroshige was born in Yedo into the Hikeshi Doshin (fire brigade) guild. As a brigadier of this guild he became a river inspector in the Tokaido district. This occupation had a great influence on his art as he constantly sketched the landscape during his frequent trips to the river stations. These sketches formed the basis of his "Fifty-three pictures of the Tokaido," the most important series of prints he produced.

Hiroshige's art in Japan approximates somehow the position of the impressionists in Western art history. His prints are spontaneous both in style and in atmosphere, capturing the essence of the fleeting moments of nature.

I think it is worth mentioning that there were three Hiroshiges. After Hiroshige's death two more artists took up his name and imitated his style. Therefore, in order to authenticate a Hiroshige print it is important to check the date.

JEAN BAPTISTE CAMILLE COROT, *Souvenir d'Italie*. ETCHING, $12\frac{1}{2}$ x $9\frac{11}{32}$. BEQUEST OF
MRS. H. O. HAVEMAYER, METROPOLITAN MUSEUM OF ART, NEW YORK.

Jean Baptiste Camille Corot

1796–1875, FRENCH

Corot, the great painter of the Barbizon school, is an interesting example of how changing taste influences the historic evaluation of an artist. Corot became famous with his later period—soft, atmospheric landscapes. At the turn of the century, his early Italian landscapes and his figure painting were ignored and examples could be bought cheaply. Then a reversal set in. The more structural Italian period is sought after by collectors and museums and simultaneously Corot was discovered as a first-rate painter of figures. To this we could add that although Corot is little known as a graphic artist he produced some of the most sensitive and personal landscape prints in the nineteenth century.

JEAN BAPTISTE CAMILLE COROT, *Environs de Rome*. ETCHING. 12⅜ X 9⅜. BEQUEST OF MRS. H. O. HAVEMAYER, METROPOLITAN MUSEUM OF ART, NEW YORK.

ODILON REDON, *The Devil* (FROM FLAUBERT'S *Temptation of St. Anthony*). LITHOGRAPH, 10 X 7⅞. GIFT OF ABBY ALDRICH ROCKEFELLER, MUSEUM OF MODERN ART, NEW YORK.

Odilon Redon

1840–1916, FRENCH

Redon was a student of Jerome and Gustave Moreau. He started to make prints under the influence of Bresdin with whom he felt spiritual affinity. His graphic work—some etchings, but mostly lithographs—consists of 206 prints. Like Bresdin he was a mystic and felt close to the literary work of Poe, Baudelaire, Flaubert, and Huysman. He was a symbolist and his fantastic imagery had great influence on the surrealists.

Although it is obvious that one cannot neglect the strange dream-world of Redon, to concentrate only on this facet of his *oeuvre* is to do a great disservice to him as an artist. One is apt to forget that Redon was an unusually sensitive and original colorist and a superb draftsman. I purposely selected, beside his "typical" prints, one lesser known portrait, to show another side of his remarkable talent.

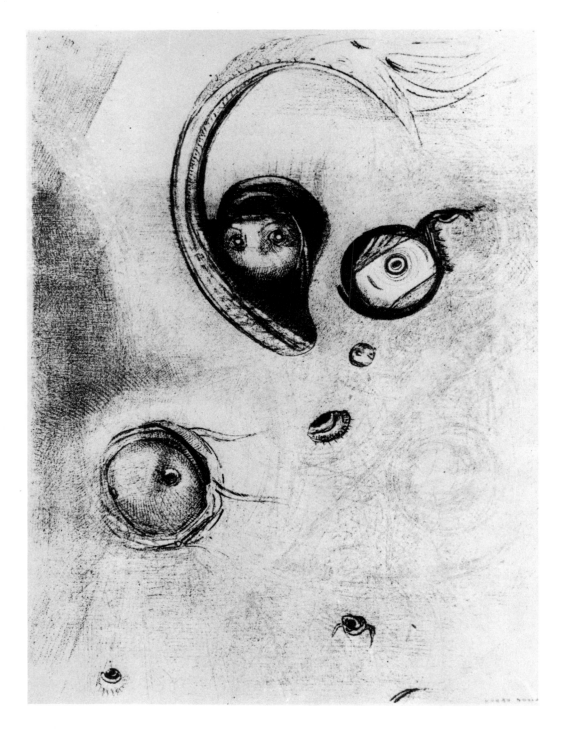

ODILON REDON, *And eyes without heads floated like mollusks* (FROM FLAUBERT'S *Temptation of St. Anthony*). LITHOGRAPH, $12\frac{1}{4}$ x $8\frac{7}{8}$. GIFT OF ABBY ALDRICH ROCKEFELLER, MUSEUM OF MODERN ART, NEW YORK.

ODILON REDON, *Pierre Bonnard*. LITHOGRAPH, 5¾ x 4⅝. LARRY ALDRICH FUND, MUSEUM OF MODERN ART, NEW YORK.

CHARLES MERYON, *Le Petit Pont*. ETCHING, 10$\frac{1}{16}$ x 7$\frac{3}{8}$. YALE UNIVERSITY ART GALLERY, NEW
HAVEN.

Charles Meryon
1821–1868, FRENCH

Meryon is, like Bresdin, a strange, eccentric figure, not representative of any school. A series of etchings on Paris is his major work. These moody prints are powerfully drawn, rich in color, and the best of them combine an air of mystery with morbid poetry.

RUDOLPHE BRESDIN, *The Holy Family Beside a Stream.* LITHOGRAPH, 9 X 7. W. S. BREWSTER
COLLECTION, ART INSTITUTE OF CHICAGO.

Rodolphe Bresdin
1822–1885, French

Bresdin was a solitary mystic, unappreciated and misunderstood most of his life. Art critics and fellow artists ingored him, with the exception of Odilon Redon who himself was a mystic. Bresdin's strange visions had more appeal to poets and he was admired by both Victor Hugo and Charles Baudelaire. Bresdin was a restless dreamer who, in search for the "ideal country" of his imagination, traveled to America and Canada. He died in France, alone and forgotten. In 1931, the Chicago Art Institute organized the first comprehensive exhibition of his work. Since then his fame has gradually increased and by now even his native France accepts him as a great artist.

I find Bresdin's work deeply moving. His position in the history of graphic arts is similar to that of Seghers. They come from the same family but their relation is spiritual rather than aesthetic. As Bresdin's work is still far less known than it deserves to be, I included in this book a representative selection of his greatest prints.

RUDOLPHE BRESDIN, *The Good Samaritan*. LITHOGRAPH, 22⅝ x 17¾. W. S. BREWSTER COL-
LECTION, ART INSTITUTE OF CHICAGO.

RUDOLPHE BRESDIN, *The Good Samaritan*. LITHOGRAPH. DETAIL. ART INSTITUTE OF CHICAGO.

RUDOLPHE BRESDIN, *The Forest of Fontainebleau.* ETCHING, 9 X 7. W. S. BREWSTER COLLECTION,
ART INSTITUTE OF CHICAGO.

RUDOLPHE BRESDIN, *The Comedy of Death*. LITHOGRAPHIC TRANSFER FROM ETCHING, 8½ x 6.
W. S. BREWSTER COLLECTION, ART INSTITUTE OF CHICAGO.

HONORÉ DAUMIER, *Je n'ai jamais tant ri* (FROM "SOUVENIRS D'ARTISTES"). LITHOGRAPH, 8 X
10⅝. BROOKLYN MUSEUM.

Honoré Daumier

1808–1879, FRENCH

Daumier is one of the greatest political satirists in the history of the graphic arts. He is the first major artist who worked nearly exclusively in lithography. Daumier was twenty years old when Goya died. The aging Goya made a few prints with the newly invented technique, but it was Daumier who explored and exploited lithography to its full potentiality. Daumier belongs to that rare breed of artists like Goya, Callot, Posada, and Picasso, whose political passions are equaled by the visual power of their work. Daumier produced over four thousand lithographs, many of them quickly made illustrations for newspaper publication. Thus, his work is very uneven in quality, but at his best he ranks with the greatest masters of the graphic arts.

HONORÉ DAUMIER, *Madeleine-Bastille*. LITHOGRAPH, $9\frac{1}{2}$ x $8\frac{5}{8}$. BROOKLYN MUSEUM.

ÉDOUARD MANET, *Guerre Civile*. LITHOGRAPH, $11\frac{5}{8}$ X $19\frac{7}{8}$. BROOKLYN MUSEUM.

Édouard Manet

1832–1883, FRENCH

The great French impressionist painter made seventy-five etchings and approximately twenty lithographs. Next to Degas, Manet was unquestionably the finest draftsman of the impressionist school. Although many of his etchings are rather dull reproductions of his paintings, some of the quickly and directly drawn portraits and figure studies are the revelations of a true master.

Except for a few short trips, Degas lived in Paris all his life. He was one of the greatest draftsmen, in the company of Hokusai, Leonardo, Ingres, and a few others. Beside his paintings, pastels, and countless drawings, Degas left a respectable number of etchings and a few drypoints. He also experimented a great deal with monoprints. Some of these are true masterpieces of startling freshness and originality.

EDGAR DEGAS, *Manet en Buste*. ETCHING, 5 x 4⅛. GIFT OF MRS. IRME DE VEGH, METROPOLITAN MUSEUM OF ART, NEW YORK.

EDGAR DEGAS, *Self-portrait*. ETCHING, 9 x 5⅝. ROSENWALD COLLECTION, NATIONAL GALLERY
OF ART, WASHINGTON, D.C.

Hilaire Germain Edgar Degas

1834–1917, FRENCH

Degas' technical knowledge of etching was rather shaky and his plates often show a lack of control over his media (foul bites, over- or under-etched areas, etc.). In spite of this, because of superb draftsmanship and unerring instinct he produced great prints. Degas is a good example of how a great artist can dominate a craft and even exploit its weaknesses, to communicate with it.

EDGAR DEGAS, *Sortie de Bain*. ETCHING, DRYPOINT. 5$\frac{1}{32}$ X 5$\frac{1}{16}$. HARRIS BRISBANE DICK FUND, METROPOLITAN MUSEUM OF ART, NEW YORK.

PAUL GAUGUIN, *Mahana Atua*. WOODCUT, 7⅜ x 8¼. CLARENCE BUCKINGHAM COLLECTION,
ART INSTITUTE OF CHICAGO.

Paul Gauguin

1848–1903, FRENCH

Gauguin, the great French postimpressionist painter was also one of the important influences on contemporary printmaking. His boldly cut, simple but powerful wood blocks not only influenced the Fauves but also greatly contributed to the graphic art of the German expressionists. Most of his color prints are dominated by the black key block. He used color sparingly, only to heighten the dramatic or poetic content of his images. Gauguin didn't treat color in a structural way and his printing varies so much from proof to proof that one could also consider them as monoprints. After his death his prints were republished with color blocks added to them. One can easily spot these prints because the color is flat and decorative and even the printing of the black key block lacks the sensitive variations of Gauguin's own handrubbing.

PAUL GAUGUIN, *Te Atua*. WOODCUT, 8⅛ x 14³⁄₁₆. WILLIAM MCCALLIN MCKEE MEMORIAL COLLECTION, ART INSTITUTE OF CHICAGO.

JAMES WHISTLER, *Dance-Rousse* (FROM THE "NOCTURNES"). ETCHING, 10½ x 6⁷⁄₁₆. HARRIS
BRISBANE DICK FUND, METROPOLITAN MUSEUM OF ART, NEW YORK.

James Abbot McNeill Whistler

1834–1903, AMERICAN

Whistler was a controversial figure, both in his art and in his personal life. He lived in Europe from 1851 and became the friend of Degas and Legros. He had legendary verbal fencings with the equally caustic Oscar Wilde.

Whistler was a successful portrait painter, but his original talent and imagination revealed itself more in his landscapes and nearly abstract mood paintings, the "Nocturnes."

Whistler was very much involved in printmaking. He made many etchings and some drypoints. He developed a lyrical, painterly style in his prints and many consider his etchings of Venice a turning point in the printmaking of the nineteenth century.

JAMES WHISTLER, *Two Doorways*. ETCHING, 8 X 11½. LIBRARY OF CONGRESS, WASHINGTON, D.C.

HENRI DE TOULOUSE-LAUTREC, *Au Moulin Rouge*. COLOR LITHOGRAPH, 18¼ x 13½.
BROOKLYN MUSEUM.

Henri de Toulouse-Lautrec

1864–1901, FRENCH

Lautrec is such a legendary figure of nineteenth-century Parisian bohemia that I don't want to waste space telling about his life. Many books, even a fairly recent film, have romanticized the life of this unhappy genius.

Lautrec was a great artist, one of the greatest draftsmen of his time. He was also one of the most instrumental figures in the revival of creative printmaking. He was definitely influenced and inspired by the Japanese color woodcut although the bulk of his graphic work was in lithography. He made over three hundred of them, including many posters, and explored this media's potential deeper than anyone before him.

Few men could draw as expressively as Lautrec. His line seems to respond to every nuance he wanted to communicate. It had an incredible quality of speed and immediacy but never appeared automatic. Unfortunately, his style was overexploited by contemporary commercial art and his witty often sarcastic spirit turned into vulgar mannerism.

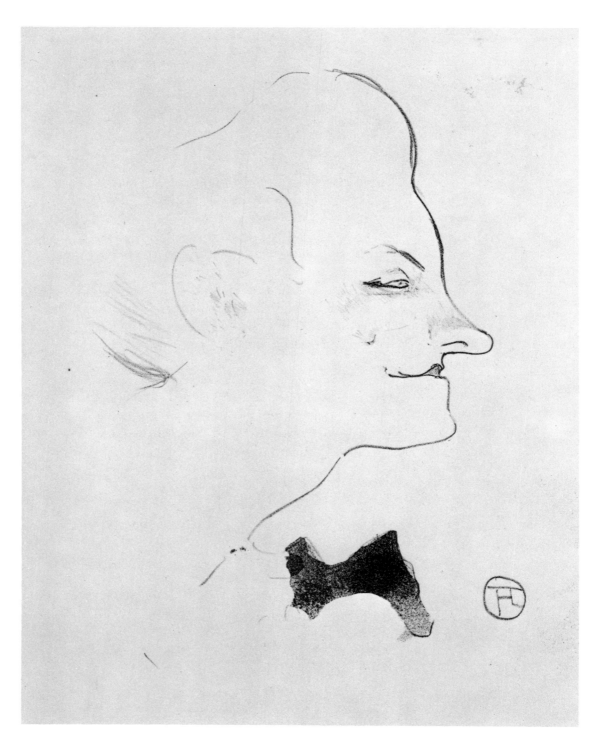

HENRI DE TOULOUSE-LAUTREC, *Yvette Guilbert*. LITHOGRAPH, $9\frac{1}{2}$ x $7\frac{5}{8}$. HARRIS BRISBANE DICK FUND, METROPOLITAN MUSEUM OF ART, NEW YORK.

HENRI DE TOULOUSE-LAUTREC, *Le Jockey*. LITHOGRAPH, 20⅜ X 14¼. HARRIS BRISBANE
DICK FUND, METROPOLITAN MUSEUM OF ART, NEW YORK.

JOSÉ GUADALUPE POSADA, *Calaveras de Gatas y Garbancereas*. RELIEF ENGRAVING ON LEAD,
4½ x 7. BROOKLYN MUSEUM.

José Guadalupe Posada

1852–1913, MEXICAN

Posada was the child of a German mother and a Mexican father. He was an illustrator, and most of his plates were cut directly into wood or lead for newspaper reproductions. His enormous output is a living document of the great popular revolution of Mexico. Posada's style is a strange mixture of sophistication with the naïveté of popular art. Most of his work did not intend to have any pretension as "art." It became art by his personal vision and plastic strength. Posada was discovered by the young artists of the revolution like Rivera and Orozko, and exercised a great influence on the development of the popular Mexican style. Unfortunately, this style eventually deteriorated into superficial mannerism and produced the arid social conscious nationalist school.

JOSÉ GUADALUPE POSADA, *Coloquie de Buenas Calaveras*. RELIEF ENGRAVING ON LEAD. EN-LARGED FROM 3⅛ x 2¼. BROOKLYN MUSEUM.

EDVARD MUNCH, *Nude with Red Hair.* 1901. LITHOGRAPH, $27\frac{3}{8}$ x $15\frac{13}{16}$. GIFT OF JAMES
THRALL SOBY, MUSEUM OF MODERN ART, NEW YORK.

Edvard Munch

1863–1944, NORWEGIAN

Munch was born near Loten and started his career in Oslo. In 1889 he went to Paris and there he made contact with the impressionists. Although this influence helped to liberate him, his painting developed in an expressionist direction with eerie psychological undertones. He made many prints, and became one of the important influences on contemporary printmaking. Munch was particularly influential on the development of color, woodcut, and color lithography.

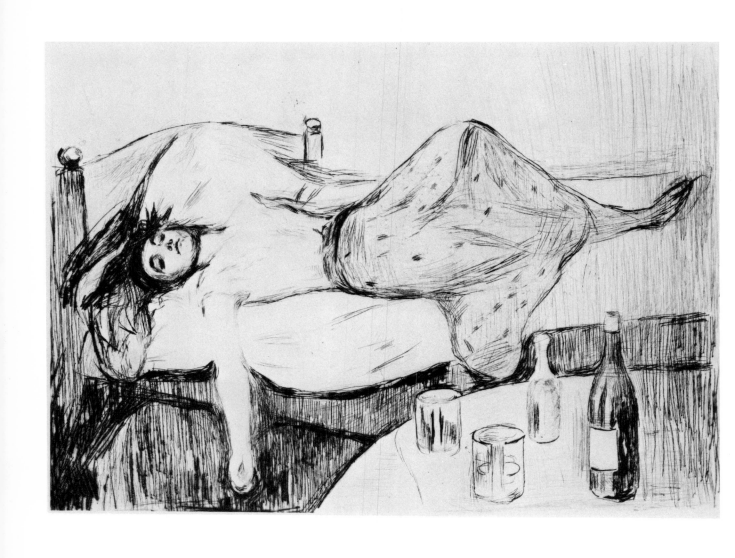

EDVARD MUNCH, *The Day After*. DRYPOINT. LIBRARY OF CONGRESS, WASHINGTON, D.C.

EDVARD MUNCH, *The Kiss.* 1902. COLOR WOODCUT, 18¼ x 18¼. MUSEUM OF MODERN ART,
NEW YORK.

JAMES ENSOR, *The Entrance of Christ into Brussels*. 1898. ETCHING, 9¾ x 14. ALDRICH ROCKEFEL-
LER FUND, MUSEUM OF MODERN ART, NEW YORK.

James Ensor

1860–1949, BELGIAN

Ensor is a very interesting figure who occupies a special niche in the history of art of the twentieth century. Stylistically he is part of the impressionist tradition but his fantastic and sometimes macabre imagery go back to Bosch and Breughel. As a painter he was a supreme and personal colorist and this is felt even in his graphic work. Ensor's visionary imagery, interpreted in a manner that we generally identify with a pastoral and lyrical attitude toward nature, gives his prints a completely unique quality.

JAMES ENSOR, *Stars at the Cemetery*. ETCHING, AQUATINT. 5½ x 7⅟₁₆. GIFT OF MRS. JOHN D. ROCKEFELLER, JR., MUSEUM OF MODERN ART, NEW YORK.

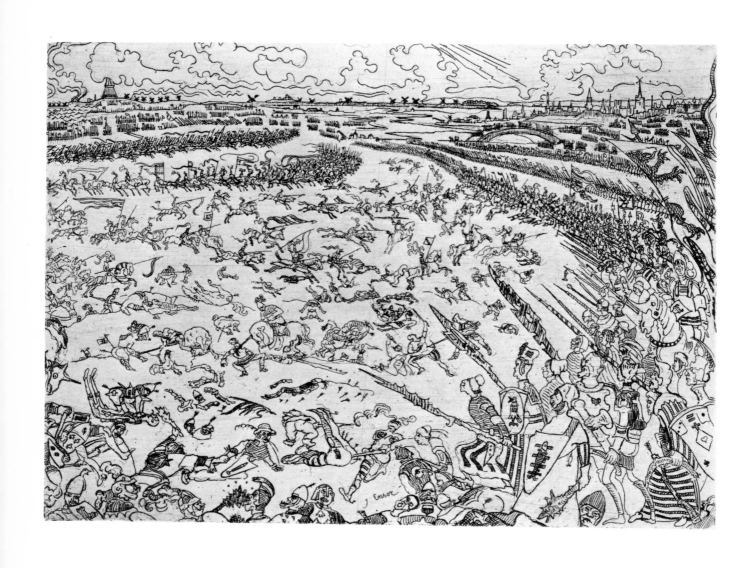

JAMES ENSOR, *The Battle of the Golden Spurs.* 1895. ETCHING, 7$\frac{1}{16}$ x 9$\frac{7}{16}$. MUSEUM OF MODERN
ART, NEW YORK.

JAMES ENSOR, *The Cathedral*. 1886. ETCHING, 9¾ x 7½. GIFT OF ABBY ALDRICH ROCKEFELLER,
MUSEUM OF MODERN ART, NEW YORK

LOVIS CORINTH, DRYPOINT FROM PORTFOLIO "AM WALTCHENSEE," 16½ x 14¼. BROOKLYN
MUSEUM.

Lovis Corinth

1858–1925, GERMAN

Corinth was an interesting transitional figure from nineteenth-century naturalism into the twentieth-century German expressionist movement. Even in his early naturalist work one can feel a subdued expressionist temperament that in his late period erupts like a volcano. Corinth's work was always uneven. He made many really bad things, but at his best he had amazing powers. He was an outstanding draftsman and he was certainly one of the finest German printmakers of his generation. Corinth made woodcuts, lithographs, etchings, and drypoints. I am particularly fond of his drypoints as this medium responded best to his energy and passionate temperament.

LOVIS CORINTH, *Death and the Artist.* 1921. SOFT GROUND ETCHING AND DRYPOINT. 9⅜ x 7.
GIFT OF J. B. NEUMAN, MUSEUM OF MODERN ART, NEW YORK.

KÄTHE KOLLWITZ, *Self-Portrait.* 1938. LITHOGRAPH. 18¾ x 11¼. MUSEUM OF MODERN ART, NEW YORK.

Käthe Kollwitz

1867–1945, German

Käthe Kollwitz was the conscience of the twentieth century. She was the visual spokesman for all women who lost their children or men in war. She protested against war, cruelty, hunger, and indifference. All this of course would make her a great human being but not necessarily a great artist. On the contrary, her emotional involvement was so intense that only her powerful draftsmanship and discipline saved her prints from the morass of sentimentality. She worked both in etching and lithography. The market is flooded with reprints of her work, some of them signed by her daughter.

ERNST BARLACH, *God Over the City* (FROM "METAMORPHIC CREATIONS OF GOD"). 1921. WOOD-CUT, 12⅞ X 17¾. GIFT OF VICTOR S. RIESENFELD, MUSEUM OF MODERN ART, NEW YORK.

Ernst Barlach

1870–1938, GERMAN

Barlach is considered the most important German sculptor of the twentieth century. In addition to being a great sculptor Barlach was also one of the best graphic artists of his time. Although he made some lithographs in his youth he is primarily appreciated for his woodcuts. It is easily understandable that a sculptor who did a great deal of wood carving felt more affinity to the woodcut. The resistance of the wood was more sympathetic to his monumental simplicity than the fluidity of the lithograph.

A great number of the Barlach woodcuts were illustrations to the plays he wrote, but he also illustrated Goethe's "Walpurgisnacht" and Schiller's "Ode to Joy." In many respects Barlach was the German counterpart of Rouault. Both were deeply religious. While Rouault was inspired by the stained glass windows of medieval cathedrals Barlach was influenced by the Gothic form. In spite of this, he was not an eclectic; he assimilated completely this influence and projected it in contemporary terms. He was a great humanist, and next to Kollwitz the most compassionate German artist of our time.

GEORGE GROSZ, *The Germans to the Front*. 1920 LITHOGRAPH, 15 x 12⅝₁₆. MUSEUM OF MODERN ART, NEW YORK.

George Grosz

1893–1959, GERMAN

Grosz was closely related to the German expressionist movement and the liberal left of the post-First-World-War-era. Between the first and the second world wars he produced a series of drawings and prints violently attacking German militarism, the moral decay that followed the war, and the exploitation of power. During this period Grosz developed a graphic style of his own. With a delicate, nearly fragile line he could evoke images of savage power. Although after his immigration to America the quality of Grosz's work declined, his earlier work ranks him as one of the great graphic artists of our time.

ERNEST LUDWIG KIRCHNER, *Dr. F. Bauer.* 1933. COLOR WOODCUT, 19¾ x 13¾. MUSEUM
OF MODERN ART, NEW YORK.

Ernest Ludwig Kirchner

1880–1938, GERMAN

Kirchner was one of the most important figures of the German expressionist movement. His morbid, often unpleasant images are the plastic documents of Germany between two disastrous wars. Even when seemingly gay, Kirchner's paintings are full of an air of impending disaster.

I like Kirchner's prints far better than his paintings. There is a directness and a precision in his prints that makes them pulsate with life, while his paintings often look dated. He made woodcuts, lithographs, and etchings. His woodcut portraits are remarkable both for their fluid draftsmanship and their psychological insight. Another side of his sensibility is revealed through his sensuous and seductive color lithographs.

ERNEST LUDWIG KIRCHNER, *Head of L. Schames.* 1917. WOODCUT, 22 X 10. MRS. JOHN D. ROCKEFELLER FUND, MUSEUM OF MODERN ART, NEW YORK.

EMIL NOLDE, *Discussion*. 1913. LITHOGRAPH, PRINTED IN COLOR, 29⁷⁄₁₆ X 23¼. MUSEUM OF
MODERN ART, NEW YORK.

Emil (Hansen) Nolde

1867–1956, GERMAN

Emil Nolde was the solitary genius of German expressionism. Although his name is closely associated with the Die Brucke group, he was a member for only a year and a half. Later, with most of the young expressionists, he was part of the New Secession movement, but not for long. He was too much of an individualist to accept the discipline of any group. While most of the German expressionists were motivated by a strong social consciousness and by humanism, the two passions of Nolde were nature and religion. Nolde's passion was savage. Next to him the violence of the other expressionists seems tame. His direct and completely spontaneous working method (even his woodcuts were started without any preliminary drawings) made him a very uneven artist who could produce both great and terrible work. Although Nolde came fairly late to graphic work, he produced an impressive number of woodcuts, etchings, and lithographs.

EMIL NOLDE, *Prophet*. 1912. WOODCUT, 15⅝ x 8¾. GIVEN ANONYMOUSLY, MUSEUM OF MODERN ART, NEW YORK.

Max Beckmann

1884–1950, GERMAN

Painter, printmaker, Beckmann was born in Leipzig, died in New York. He was one of the powerful figures of the German expressionist movement. A great draftsman, his personal, brutally strong drawing dominated even his painting. His lines drawn on paper or on canvas looked like incisions into hard rock with a dull chisel. Like most German expressionists he made many woodcuts, also a number of drypoints. I am particularly fond of the latter as the immediacy of the scratched line responded admirably to Beckmann's virile draftsmanship.

MAX BECKMANN, *Self-Portrait with Bowler Hat.* DRYPOINT, 12¾ x 9¾. GIFT OF EDWARD M. WARBURG, MUSEUM OF MODERN ART, NEW YORK.

MAX BECKMANN, *Adam and Eve*. 1917. DRYPOINT, 9¾ x 6¹⁵⁄₁₆. LARRY ALDRICH FUND,
MUSEUM OF MODERN ART, NEW YORK.

Edward Hopper

1882–1966, AMERICAN

Hopper occupies a very special position in American art. He worked outside of the mainstream of twentieth-century art, untouched and uninterested in the formalistic experimentation of his contemporaries. He wasn't an innovator, but in his hard-boiled, silent landscapes he projected something uniquely American, like the poetry of Robert Frost.

Hopper's figures are still, lonely props completely overwhelmed by the superhuman scale of their environment. He isn't too well known as a printmaker, yet his etchings are masterful and just as expressive as his paintings.

EDWARD HOPPER, *American Landscape*. 1921. ETCHING, $7\frac{7}{16}$ X $12\frac{7}{16}$. GIFT OF ABBY ALDRICH ROCKEFELLER, MUSEUM OF MODERN ART, NEW YORK.

GEORGES ROUAULT, *Face to Face* (FROM THE "MISERERE"). AQUATINT, DRYPOINT, AND ROU-LETTE. $22\frac{11}{16}$ X $17\frac{3}{16}$. GIFT OF THE ARTIST, MUSEUM OF MODERN ART, NEW YORK.

Georges Rouault

1871–1958, FRENCH

One can't put Rouault into any school of painting. He was a student of Gustave Moreau, but his paintings, fortunately, show none of this influence. He was associated with the Fauves in Paris, but stylistically had very little to do with them. Some people classify him as an expressionist, but I prefer to think of him as a religious painter who was probably more influenced by Byzantine mosaics and medieval stained-glass windows than anything contemporary.

Rouault made many prints, most of them published by Vollard. His most famous set is the "Miserere," published in 1948. This series of large etchings depicting the life of Christ is one of the most powerful graphic statements of our time. His unorthodox method of making them created a lot of controversy. Most of these plates are reworked photogravures after wash drawings especially made for this purpose.

GEORGES ROUAULT, *Verlaine*. 1933. LITHOGRAPH, 2D STATE, 17 X 12¾. BROOKLYN MUSEUM.

GIORGIO MORANDI, *Still Life with Coffeepot*. 1933. ETCHING, 11$\frac{11}{16}$ X 15$\frac{3}{8}$. MRS. BERTRAM
SMITH FUND, MUSEUM OF MODERN ART, NEW YORK.

Giorgio Morandi

1890–1964, ITALIAN

Where is Morandi's place in contemporary art? Who knows? While the whole world was going wild with innovations, inventions, and revolutions, Morandi kept on painting small, lyrical landscapes and still lifes—all kinds of bottles, little ones and big ones, fat and lean, light and dark ones. His is a silent, intimate world, where time stands still. It is a nice place to go out of this noisy world. He made many prints, mostly small etchings; modest little plates, companions of his paintings. They are intimate and understated like the chamber music of a master.

GIORGIO MORANDI, *Still Life*. 1945. ETCHING, 10½ X 11¾. MUSEUM OF MODERN ART, NEW YORK.

PAUL KLEE, *The Hero with the Wing*. 1905. ETCHING, 9⅛ x 5¾. MUSEUM OF MODERN ART, NEW YORK.

Paul Klee

1879–1940, Swiss

Klee has a very special place in the art of the twentieth century. It is impossible to put him into any category. He was associated with the Bauhaus, but was never a Bauhaus painter; he used some of the formal devices of cubism but he never was a cubist. He was a wit and a poet. He was inventive, but in such a personal way that nobody could use his inventions profitably without becoming his imitator. To the young artists of today his sensibility is too subtle, his poetry too romantic, but I am sure that he will survive as one of the great artists of our time. Klee made approximately 120 plates, many of them revealing the same sensitivity and inventiveness as his paintings.

PAUL KLEE, *Jugler in April*. 1928. ETCHING, 7½ x 7⅝. MUSEUM OF MODERN ART, NEW YORK.

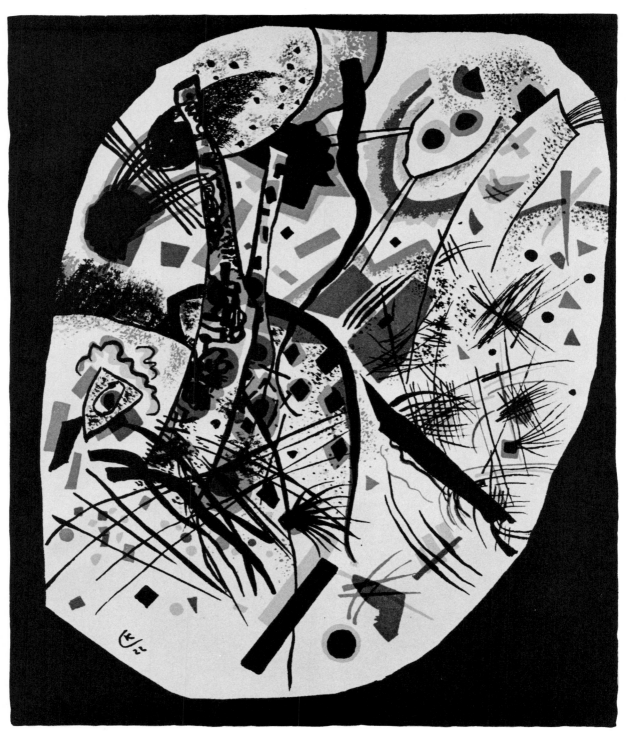

VASILI KANDINSKI, *Abstraction* (FROM "KLEINE WELTEN"). 1922. LITHOGRAPH, 10$\frac{15}{16}$ X 9$\frac{1}{16}$. GIFT OF ABBY ALDRICH ROCKEFELLER, MUSEUM OF MODERN ART, NEW YORK.

Vasili Kandinski

1866–1944, RUSSIAN

Kandinski was born in Russia but spent most of his life in Germany, where he was one of the most influential members of the Bauhaus, and his last years in Paris.

He was one of the great innovators of twentieth-century art and strangely enough, while his geometric abstractions exercised strong influence on the development of contemporary "hard edge" painting, his earlier free abstractions heralded the coming of abstract expressionism.

Kandinsky's woodcuts and lithographs are the forceful and personal expressions of a great artist.

VASILI KANDINSKI, *Abstraction*. WOODCUT, ENGRAVING, 9½ x 8½. BROOKLYN MUSEUM.

MARC CHAGALL, FROM THE BIBLE. ETCHING, 1 1¾ x 9½. BROOKLYN MUSEUM.

Marc Chagall

1887–   , RUSSIAN

Chagall's world is a strange mixture of naive, poetic imagery related to his Russian-Jewish origin, coupled with a sophisticated *école de Paris* painterly culture. The marriage of these two contradictory elements produces the particular seductiveness of Chagall's imagery. During his long productive life he produced an impressive body of graphic work, both etchings and lithographs. He illustrated many books; *The Dead Souls* by Gogol and the Bible are his outstanding contributions in this field. Although nearly eighty years old he still produces both paintings and prints in great quantities. Unfortunately, under the constant pressure of public demand, his late work has become a commercial parody of his earlier genuine poetry.

MARC CHAGALL, *Self-Portrait with Grimace*. C.1924–25. ETCHING WITH AQUATINT, 14 X 10. GIFT OF THE ARTIST, MUSEUM OF MODERN ART, NEW YORK.

PIERRE BONNARD, *The Bath*. 1924. LITHOGRAPH, 11¾ x 9½. MUSEUM OF MODERN ART, NEW
YORK.

Pierre Bonnard

1867–1947, FRENCH

Bonnard, together with Vuillard, Denis, and Suzanne Valotton formed the Nabis, a small group of artists bound together more by common ideals than aesthetics. Bonnard was certainly one of the greatest colorists of the postimpressionist period.

Bonnard's position in contemporary painting is rather interesting. He painted out of the impressionist tradition but, by pushing way beyond it he bridged the nineteenth and the twentieth centuries. While the impressionists used color to create light, toward the end of his life, Bonnard used light to dramatize color.

As Bonnard was a colorist primarily, lithography was the best printmaking method to serve his sensitivities. Most of his graphic works were published by Vollard. Bonnard's graphic style was influenced by the Japanese color woodcut, simple areas of color dramatized by unexpected change of pace, from the most delicate details to the explosively bold.

Bonnard also made a few etchings and drypoints. As his lithographs are so often seen and reproduced, I selected, also, one of his etchings for reproduction. This portrait of the old Renoir crippled by arthritis, drawn with simplicity and directness, is a tender, moving human document.

PIERRE BONNARD, *Portrait of A. Renoir*. 1914. ETCHING, DRYPOINT. 10⅛ x 7¾. MUSEUM OF MODERN ART, NEW YORK.

ÉDOUARD VUILLARD, *La Cuisiniere*. LITHOGRAPH, 14⅛ X 10¾. BROOKLYN MUSEUM.

Jean Édouard Vuillard

1868–1940, FRENCH

Vuillard is always closely associated with the great friend of his youth, Bonnard. They both belonged to the Nabis group and both were, in spite of this, strongly influenced by the Japanese color woodcut. However, they both worked in lithography and not in woodcut. The oriental influence in their work manifests itself more in the color and space concept than in actual style.

Vuillard made fifty-two color lithographs between 1893 and 1914. These landscapes and *interieurs* are truly amazing. They are fresh, vibrant, and very abstract in concept. Looking at them one feels sorry that Vuillard, in his later periods, became obsessively involved with naturalistic representation that somehow robbed his painting of spark and color. In view of their close association, it is interesting that while the aging Bonnard became increasingly abstract, the old Vuillard became illustrative.

HENRI MATISSE, *Head with the Eyes Closed*. 1906. LITHOGRAPH, $17\frac{5}{16}$ X $10\frac{12}{16}$. GIFT OF ABBY ALDRICH ROCKEFELLER, MUSEUM OF MODERN ART, NEW YORK.

Henri Matisse

1869–1954, FRENCH

Matisse was, without any question, one of the greatest artists of the twentieth century. He was a great painter, a great sculptor, and an outstanding draftsman. He was truly a complete artist.

Matisse left behind him an impressive graphic *oeuvre*, nearly five hundred prints. He illustrated many books. Although Matisse made some etchings and a few woodcuts, the majority of his graphic work was in lithography. Matisse was one of those rare artists who could make extremely complex things look very simple. His line is a miracle of precision and sensitivity. With the simplest thread of line Matisse could evoke form, space, color, light, and motion.

HENRI MATISSE, *Reclining Nude with Stove*. 1928–29. LITHOGRAPH, 22 x 18⅛. GIFT OF ABBY
ALDRICH ROCKEFELLER. MUSEUM OF MODERN ART, NEW YORK.

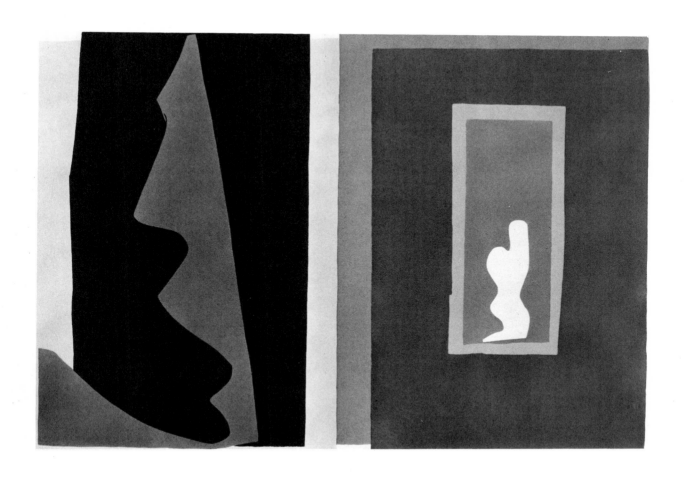

HENRI MATISSE, *Desting* (FROM "THE JAZZ SERIES"). 1947. SERIGRAPH, 16¼ X 25. GIFT OF THE ARTIST, MUSEUM OF MODERN ART, NEW YORK.

JACQUES VILLON, *J. P. Dubray*. 1933. ETCHING, ENGRAVING. 10⅞ x 8³⁄₁₆. MUSEUM OF
MODERN ART, NEW YORK.

Jacques Villon

1875–1963, FRENCH

Villon is one of the most important influences on contemporary printmaking. He started out as a commercial engraver and at the beginning of his career made many reproductions of other artists' work. Some of these colored aquatints are miracles of craftsmanship. In 1911 he stopped his commercial work and joined the cubist movement. His serious graphic work began after his return from the war in 1914. He set to work on a series of engravings primarily preoccupied with space structure and light created by the overlapping web of lines. This approach was characteristic of most of his graphic work.

In the thirties Villon started a long series of color prints using intaglio lithography and wood, sometimes in combination. In his later life he painted more and more, but in spite of the fact that he was known and appreciated by fellow artists most of his life, he was in his seventies when finally the long deserved international fame came to him. Villon was a great poet of color and light.

Not long before his death he told a friend of his: "The secret is to out-live them."

JOAN MIRÓ, *Le chien aboyant a la Lune* (FROM *Verve*). LITHOGRAPH, 14¼ x 21⅜. LARRY ALD-
RICH FUND, MUSEUM OF MODERN ART, NEW YORK.

Joan Miró

1893–   , SPANISH

Miró lives in a very special world. It is funny, it is sad, it is childish but very sophisticated. It always seems to laugh, but it is very serious. He created this world for himself and for anyone who is willing to take a trip with him.

His imagery, the floating, dancing organic shapes, his strange trailing lines, even his color sense, is ideally suited for the print. He is one of the most prolific graphic artists of our time. He works in every medium, color woodcut, etching, drypoint, lithograph, silkscreen, and he also combines many of these. Although he is considered primarily as an important painter, not long ago he received the graphic prize at the Venice Biennial.

JOAN MIRÓ, *Composition*. ETCHING, 10 X 9. GIFT OF VICTOR S. RIESENFELD. MUSEUM OF MODERN ART, NEW YORK.

PABLO PICASSO, *Head of a Boy*. 1945. LITHOGRAPH, 12¼ x 9⅜. CURT VALENTIN BEQUEST, MUSEUM OF MODERN ART, NEW YORK.

Pablo Ruiz y Picasso

1881–   , SPANISH

It is a hopeless task to write a biographical sketch of Picasso within a few lines. What could one say that has not already been said in the countless books and articles published about him? He is not an artist, he is a phenomenon. I doubt that any man ever stamped his image on his time to the extent Picasso has done. He was the white knight of contemporary art's heroic period. He created many styles, painted thousands of pictures, made thousands of drawings, prints, ceramics, and made hundreds of sculptures. To me he is primarily a great graphic artist and a great sculptor. I don't think that he is as great a colorist as Matisse or Bonnard. Picasso's main strength is always structure and line. His painting reproduces well in black and white, Matisse's painting rarely, and Bonnard's never.

Picasso's graphic work is truly staggering, both in quantity and in quality. He has worked in every medium but etching and lithography seem to be his favorites. In recent years he even made a series of large colored linoleum cuts, and proved again that in the hand of a great artist a technique generally associated with hobbyists and school children can become a major art form. To select a few prints out of the thousands he has produced is not easier than to pick a few Rembrandts; maybe even more difficult because any one good Rembrandt print could convey his greatness, while with Picasso one has to realize his versatility, his inexhaustible inventiveness in order to understand the full scope of his talent.

PABLO PICASSO, PLATE FROM OVID'S *Les Metamorphoses*. 1931. ETCHING, 9 x 6¾. GIFT OF JAMES THRALL SOBY, MUSEUM OF MODERN ART, NEW YORK.

PABLO PICASSO, *Bull, Horse and Woman*. 1934. ETCHING, 11$\frac{11}{16}$ x 9$\frac{5}{16}$. MUSEUM OF MODERN ART, NEW YORK.

PABLO PICASSO, *Minotoromachia*. ETCHING, 19½ x 27¼. BROOKLYN MUSEUM.

PABLO PICASSO, *Weeping Woman*. STUDY FOR *Guernica*. 1937. ETCHING, AQUATINT, 27 X 19.
LENT BY THE ARTIST, MUSEUM OF MODERN ART, NEW YORK.

PABLO PICASSO, *Toad*. 1949. LITHOGRAPH, 19⅝ x 25¼. ABBY ALDRICH ROCKEFELLER FUND, MUSEUM OF MODERN ART, NEW YORK.

PABLO PICASSO, *Minotaur and Woman*. 1933. DRYPOINT, 11⅝ X 14⅜. MUSEUM OF MODERN
ART, NEW YORK.

Bibliography

A Guide to the Collecting and Care of Original Prints, Carl Zigrosser and Christa M. Gaehde. Crown Publishers, 1965.
About Prints, S. W. Hayter. Oxford University Press, 1962.
Albrecht Dürer—Complete Woodcuts, Dr. Willi Kurth. Crown Publishers, 1946.
An Introduction to a History of Woodcut, Arthur M. Hind. (2 vol.) Dover Publications, 1963.
De-Meesterwerken van de Europese Prentkunst, catalogue. Rijksmuseum, Amsterdam, 1966.
Dürer, W. Waetzold. Phaidon Publishers, 1950.
Fine Prints, Carl Zigrosser. Crown Publishers, 1958.
Giovanni Battista Piranesi, Hyatt Mayor. H. Bittner & Co., 1952.
Graphic Arts of the Twentieth Century, Wolf Stubbe. Frederick A. Praeger, 1963.
Hercules Seghers, Leo C. Collins. University of Chicago Press, 1953.
Hokusai, I. Hillier. Phaidon Publishers, 1957.
Il Conoscitore di Stampe, Ferdinando Salamon. Giulio Einandi Ed., 1961, Italy.
Kaethe Kolwitz, George Braziller, 1951, New York.
L'Estampe par Jean Laran, Presses Universitaires de France. (2 vol.) Paris, 1959.
Masterpieces of the Japanese Color Woodcut, Willy Boller. Boston Book and Art shop.
New Ways of Gravure, S. W. Hayter. Pantheon Press, 1949.
Printmaking, Gabor Peterdi. Macmillan, 1959.
Rembrandt Etchings, Ludwig Munz. (2 vol.) Phaidon Press, 1952.
Rembrandt Gravures, K. G. Boon. Art et Metier Graphic, Paris, 1963.
Redon, Moreau, Bresdin, Museum of Modern Art, 1961.
The Complete Etchings of Goya, Crown Publishers, 1943.
The Bite of the Print, Frank and Dorothy Getlein. Clarcson N. Potter, New York, 1963.
The German Expressionists, Bernard S. Myers. Frederick A. Praeger, 1956.
Toulouse-Lautrec Lithographies, Jean Adhemar. Art and Metier Graphic, 1965.